T0248126

The First Three Years of the Child

Karl Konig with his two-year-old son,
Christof, and his daughter Renate

The First Three Years of the Child

How Children Learn to Walk, Speak and Think

Karl König

Edited by Jan Goeschel

Floris Books

Publisher's note

This book was written in the 1950s and, while some of the
language has been updated for this new edition, the content
still reflects the era and culture in which it was written.

Translated by Carlo Pietzner

Karl König Archive Publication, Vol. 22
Subject: Psychology and Education
Edited by Jan Goeschel

Series editor: Richard Steel

Karl König's collected works are issued by
the Karl König Archive, Aberdeen

First published in German as *Die ersten drei Jahre des Kindes*
by Verlag Freies Geistesleben, Stuttgart, in 1957
First published in English by Floris Books, Edinburgh, in 1984
This third edition 2023
© 1957 Verlag Freies Geistesleben
© 2023 Trustees of the Karl König Archives

All rights reserved. No part of this publication may
be reproduced without the prior permission of
Floris Books, Edinburgh
www.florisbooks.co.uk

 Also available as an eBook

British Library CIP Data available
ISBN 978-178250-847-2

Contents

Foreword

Jan Goeschel

It is a great pleasure to introduce this slightly revised and comprehensively annotated edition of Karl König's book on *The First Three Years of the Child*. In this text, the physician and founder of the Camphill Movement gives an account of the principal developmental steps of the first three years: the acquisition of upright walking, the use of language and the beginnings of thinking. Alongside these, König explores the emergence of social perception and the sensory systems that underly our ability to perceive and comprehend acts of communication: the word sense and the thought sense (our ability to understand words and concepts) as well as our sense of the embodied presence of the other human being, the other 'I'.

König does this by weaving several strands into an organic tapestry that offers an integrated picture of how these foundational human capacities emerge in early childhood. He draws on the most current findings of his time from physiology, psychology, linguistics and other related fields, as well as Rudolf Steiner's spiritual-scientific insights. Integrating what is known empirically, he always strives to go beyond a simple addition of facts, towards a living understanding of the dynamically interconnected developmental forces and processes at work. Drawing together a phenomenology of inner and outer aspects, he then looks for access to the deeper significance of these stages in the human being's journey through the body into the world of time and space. Archetypal imaginations from sacred myths become aides towards a contemplative and spiritually deepened view of what is essential in each step. And yet his understanding always remains anchored in the realities of the underlying physiological, neurodevelopmental processes.

In preparing this new edition, my goal has been to bring König's work, now more than 65 years old, into a fruitful and open-ended dialogue with contemporary scientific and scholarly perspectives. It turns out – and I hope you will agree – that König's book has aged well! Exciting new vistas, especially regarding the neurosciences which have advanced significantly since König's time, open up. Certainly, here and there, specific details can be added that were not available in the 1950s. Overall, however, the trends of the last decades are incredibly well aligned with the more visionary and, at the time, perhaps seemingly more speculative aspects of König's and Rudolf Steiner's understanding of child development: the intimately interconnected nature of movement, communication, social perception and cognition, and the phenomena of embodied resonance that underly much of this.

In trying to offer avenues of dialogue and engagement with König's text, I have decided in favour of extensive endnotes, rather than a lengthy introduction. In the original text, König used endnotes to indicate the sources of his quotes, which are included here in the original format. References to Rudolf Steiner's work include the volume numbers for either the CW (Collected Works) or the German GA (Gesamtausgabe) editions. In the Endnotes section at the back of the book, König's comments and references are marked with (KK), those marked (Ed.) are mine.

My reasons for this choosing this form for my commentary are several: König's approach is genuinely transdisciplinary, drawing on many different disciplines and fields of knowledge, from the natural sciences to theology, in the service of the theme of his investigation. An introductory essay that does justice to all these dimensions would have needed to become a transdisciplinary treatise in its own right. Instead, the endnotes allow me to comment on the text in a more open-ended way, taking the opportunity to branch out in different directions, bring context, clarify the status of current scientific thinking, point to related bodies of work that offer complementary perspectives and questions and opportunities for further research. With this in mind, I hope you will use my endnotes as a springboard to launch into your own pursuits of deeper understanding wherever they arouse your interest and curiosity.

My greatest hope would be to see such engagement with König's text lead to new publications (in whatever form, written or oral, symposia, workshops, presentations, articles, books, dissertations) that build on his seminal work and take it further. But not only in publications – I believe that König's ultimate motive as a physician and educator of children with developmental disabilities was to contribute to an understanding of child development that could help support the development of children, especially where it takes place under difficult circumstances. If this new edition can help make König's insights – which were never meant as a finished project, but to be continued by all those working with them – available to educators, therapists, physicians, caregivers, parents and all supporters of young people, and if it can lead to the development of new insights and inspiration for educational, therapeutic and social practice, then the task will have been accomplished. I hope you will enjoy working with this text as much as I have in preparing this edition.

Introduction

Karl König

During the first three years of our earthly existence we acquire those faculties that enable us to become human.[1] In the course of the first year we learn to walk, during the second we acquire speech, and during the third, we experience the awakening of thought. We are born as helpless infants and only by acquiring these three faculties of walking, speaking and thinking do we grow into individuals who can name ourselves, gain free mobility and, with the help of speech, come into conscious communication with other people in the surrounding world. A kind of threefold miracle happens because here is revealed more than instinct, more than adaptation, more than the unfolding of inherited faculties.

The acquisition of the three fundamental human faculties is an act of grace that is bestowed on every human being. It is also a process of extraordinary complexity. Only a closer study of these phenomena reveals how manifold and varied are the ways in which the whole human being is woven into this developmental process.

The following deliberations try to follow the traces on the path that leads to learning to walk, speak and think. A concluding chapter is concerned with how the interaction of these three fundamental soul faculties work into one another and are connected with the three highest senses: the senses of speech, thought and self or ego.[2]

1. Acquiring the Ability to Walk Upright

The processes of movement

The faculty of walking upright is part of the phenomenon of the whole human organisation's faculty of movement, and it is quite one-sided to assume that we use mainly our legs and feet for walking. The entire bodily apparatus of movement is used for walking and the arms are engaged as much as the legs. The muscles of the back and chest are as intimately involved as are those that move the eyeballs.

It is necessary to recognise that the whole human being is engaged in every movement they make because the movement of one part of their body presupposes the state of rest of the other parts that are not actively engaged in this movement.[1] During waking hours from morning until night, the resting condition of some parts of the body is never a passive but always an active function. This points to an archetypal phenomenon of all movement. If one part of the bodily apparatus of movement is in motion, then the remaining part is engaged in such a way that through an active state of rest the mobility of the other part is made possible.

When I bend my arm, then I must, in order to make this flexion possible, not only actively relax the extensors of the arm in question, but all other muscles must form an active abutment to counterbalance this flexion. Thus, it is always the whole motor apparatus that takes part in every movement and helps in its performance.

The involvement of the whole bodily apparatus of movement can be experienced directly when, for example, through an injury, a toe is hindered in its ability to move freely. Immediately the function of the whole foot is arrested and the movement of the leg is changed, all of which leads indirectly to a different use of the remaining motor system. How often do pains gradually occur in the muscles of the neck and spine when a foot cannot be used properly for walking, and how often can a change in the rhythm of breathing be observed when a leg must be kept quiet for a long time. These are simple examples, but they clearly show what appears as a first and fundamental phenomenon in the realm of movement. It can be formulated as follows:

1. The entire bodily apparatus of movement is a functional unity. Its elements never move as independent members, but each movement occurs in the realm of the bodily motor system.
2. Therefore, the parts in motion show merely an apparent independence in contrast to those at rest. The resting parts, however, participate as actively in the process of movement as the parts in motion, even if this is not immediately evident.

Recognition of the bodily motor organisation as a functional unity has been prevented by the dominance of the concept of localisation of the control of movement in the central nervous system. This is the result of the analytical method of scientific thinking of the nineteenth century and in our time would best be overcome.[2] As little as single letters alone give meaning to the word, or single words the sentence, just as little does a series of single muscles move a limb of the body. The pattern of a movement uses muscles singly and in groups and so the movement is made apparent. Just as, when an opinion is stated, use is made of the sentence, which in turn takes its form from spoken words, so does gesture fall into single patterns of movement that call on groups of muscles to execute what the gesture demands.

When I feel repulsion, various patterns of movement are at the disposal of this feeling. These patterns select specific groups of muscles from the whole motor apparatus and execute a movement with them in which the whole apparatus participates. Desire and repulsion, sympathy and antipathy, anger and anxiety, fear and courage, all have their corresponding forms of movement. More refined feelings and sensations such as listening and devotion, joy and pain, weeping and laughing also have gesture patterns at their disposal and service. When human beings learn to write or weave, to carve, paint, hammer, or forge, they have themselves acquired movement patterns that are their own creation. These are not given to them as part of their heritage as created beings.

The most fundamental of these acquired forms of movement, a gesture permeating the whole of human life, is the ability to walk upright. In standing erect human beings raise themselves to a position that continually demands that they come to terms with the earth's gravity. Four-legged animals are in a greater state of equilibrium with gravity, but human beings must learn to stay uninterruptedly erect. They must not only rest freely in their uprightness, but also be able to move unburdened.

How do children acquire this faculty that demands their constant personal involvement?

The development of walking

Children's ability to move does not begin after birth but already exists during foetal development. From the end of the second month of pregnancy onward, movements of the foetus can be detected, and in the course of the fifth month they become so strong that the mother can perceive them.

When they are born, children possess a general mobility from which certain specific forms of movement stand out. For example, soon after birth they can perform perfect sucking movements when the breast is offered. They can also, from the time of their birth, control their breathing. Repulsion brought about by fear causes movement, and completely aimless and uncoordinated kicking movements as expressions of well-being are distributed over the whole body. William Stern[3] describes these movements as spontaneous and points out that they occur in a dissociated fashion. 'Many newborn infants,' he writes, 'can move each eye independently of the other. One may turn up, the other out, or one may remain stationary while the other looks down.'

Stern calls attention in particular to eye movements because their coordination takes place remarkably quickly. 'It is true,' he continues, 'that this period [of dissociated eye movements] passes quickly, sometimes even at the moment of birth, so that such children appear to have been born with coordinated eye movements.'[4]

Controlled eye movements thus stand out from the general chaos of kicking movements even during the first days of life. This is the beginning, however, of the process of movement that will be completed by the end of the first year when children have learned to walk. In learning to walk they acquire their first mastery over space. But the acquisition of this faculty proceeds according to a definitely ordered sequence that starts at the head and neck and gradually extends downwards to the chest, arms, back, and finally to the legs and feet. Generally speaking, children learn to master movements of the head and neck during their first three months. During the second quarter they control lifting their arms and hands, movements that can be distinguished from general kicking. In this way, by the end of this period, they have learned to sit freely. In the third quarter, children discover their legs and begin to practise standing. During the last quarter they carry this ability to stand over into their first free steps and experience their feet as organs touching the ground. The first conquest of space has thus been completed.

The developmental process of movement, therefore, is shifted from the head down over the chest and legs into the feet, following a course through the body from above downwards. When we ask what the meaning of this is, it becomes evident that it directly conditions the erect body posture. The head is the first member to withdraw from chaotic movement. Chest and arms are pulled along after it, and finally the legs and feet extricate themselves. This process seems to be patterned after that of actual birth. Just as in the majority of births the head is the first part of the body to emerge and is gradually followed by the rest of the body, so here, out of the womb of dissociated movements, coordinated movement is born and oriented step by step towards standing and walking. At the end of the first year the process of the birth of movement is completed.

With this achievement the head is directed upwards and the feet touch the earth. The head acquires a position of rest (a fact to which Rudolf Steiner has drawn attention time and again) and is suspended lightly upon the shoulders, becoming the resting point around which the movement of the limbs can take place.

The fundamental investigations of Rudolf Magnus and Adriaan de Kleijn[5] on the attitudinal and positional reflexes have shown the central position taken by the neck and head muscles in early development.[6] The head takes an independent position of rest in order to make possible a free and harmonious mobility of the limbs. This applies especially to the ability to walk. When human beings can keep their heads upright and still, they can also learn to walk. As long as an individual's head is restless and wobbly in the totality of movement, normal walking cannot be attained.

After the first year children also learn to free their arms from the action of walking and to use them independently. This happens because the head gradually becomes fixed and consolidated in its position of rest and is able to confront the free play of the limbs independently. The head, therefore, is a centre that rests within the movements of the body.

What has been said here can be summed up as follows. Children learn to walk in stages and give birth to their motility from the head downwards out of the chaos of early movement. As a result, the head attains a position of rest as opposed to the free mobility of the limbs. Once an upright position has been achieved, the limbs must constantly come to terms with the gravitational forces of space because, as upright individuals, human beings must be able to assume a freely mobile position of equilibrium rather than one that is fixed.

Separation of self and world

It has been pointed out that coordination of eye movements is achieved immediately after birth when children acquire the first rudiments of what later becomes their ability to look. They learn to turn their eyes to definite points in the outside world.

When we consider that, in coordinating eye movements, the first fixed point in the relationship between the soul and its surroundings is established, the fundamental importance of seeing as a human act becomes still more evident. It is by means of our eyes that we try to establish a conscious relationship with our surroundings even during the first days of our earthly life. This is not to say that children can already perceive, but they begin to explore the surrounding world as it is gradually revealed by the 'touch' of their gaze. In this way a first dull sensation of the 'there' in contrast to the 'self' comes about. In the course of their first year, the dull feeling slowly brightens and gradually leads to the contrast between the sensation of their own bodies and that of the surrounding world, but the outside and inside – the 'there' and the 'here' – will still be completely interwoven.[7] Adalbert Stifter[8] has expressed this period of development in his autobiographical fragment as follows:

> Far back in the empty void, something like rapture and delight entered my being, mightily grasping it as if to destroy. I can compare it to nothing else in my later life. What I remember was glory, turmoil; it was below. This must have occurred very early in my childhood because it seems to me as if a dark nothingness, high and broad, lay around about it. Then there was something else that passed gently and soothingly through my inner being, which I can now characterise as sound. I swam in something that fanned me. I swam to and fro and it became softer and softer within me until I became as if drunk. Then there was nothing more. These demi-islands of remembrance lie in the veiled ocean of the past, fairylike and legendary, like the primeval memories of a people.[9]

Gradually children's dull consciousness, which consists of merging sense perceptions and feelings, lights up as the world becomes differentiated from their bodies. The process of differentiation starts, however, with children looking about. As their gaze gradually becomes fixed, the individual forms of the environment can be gropingly touched and grasped. Around the focus of looking, the head emerges as a structure belonging to the self. Babies learn to lift their heads and to use them as organs of orientation, turning them to where light, colour, sound or smell come to meet them.

As time goes on, children's eyes catch sight more often of their little hands and fingers playing and moving in front of them. When not only their eyes, but also their hands begin to grasp objects, holding and dropping them again, then their torsos, including arms and hands, stand out as a whole against the world. Around this time children have acquired the faculty of sitting freely and, in doing so, they have already achieved a good deal. Their heads are suspended above their bodies and can turn freely. Their eyes begin to extend their gaze further into space while their hands grasp things nearby and bring them to their mouths. Their hands can now also grasp the edges of their cradles. They can hold on to them and pull themselves up.

Then the great moment occurs when, at about the end of the ninth month, children pull themselves up without support into a sitting position for the first time. A decisive step has now been taken. Children have separated themselves out from the surrounding world, which now confronts their newly awakened selves as something alien, and they begin to move around within it by crawling, sliding and pushing. Every day and every hour new impressions appear, always quickly forgotten and always freshly conquered. These many new experiences demand to be seized, grasped, beheld and touched. The senses encourage mobility, and movement in turn conquers new sense experiences.[10] At this time, this process is quite obvious.

Now in an upright position, children can at last take their first uncertain steps. The pride of parents often cannot be compared with children's joy in what they have achieved. The world, no longer strange and uncanny, turns into something that can be conquered by a freely moving individual. By achieving their first steps, children have also taken their first steps away from being 'creatures' to becoming 'creators'. Stern expresses it as follows:

> So, towards the end of the first year, the spadework in the mastery of actual space is mainly accomplished. The child can grasp the spatial features of things – his position, distance, shape and size – and he accommodates himself to them. He distinguishes far and near, great and small, round and angular, above and below, before and behind – in short, he has roughly a perception of space, which certainly is still capable of many misconceptions and will need in years to come to be refined, made clearer and developed, but not enriched with any intrinsically new features.[11]

Perception of space comes about at the end of the first year only because children can experience above and below through the development of their ability to stand upright. They have experienced what is near and far by their movements, the round and angular through touch, and the various positions in space by sight. But all this happens only because the process of separation between self and world has been completed. Children do not learn to walk by learning to bring certain muscular movements under control. Rather, they learn to control movements through an awakening of consciousness that gradually separates their bodies from their environment as an independent self. The delivery of the body from the intimate embrace of its mothering environment leads to the ability to walk upright. Walking upright is not a simple process of movement that makes locomotion possible. Learning to walk reveals a process of developing consciousness that leads to the perception of the environment as something 'outside'. The process begins with looking, continues in grasping and culminates in walking. The awakening consciousness that enables children to comprehend their own selves at the end of the first year moves from the *gaze* of their eyes over the *grasp* of their hands to the *step* of their feet.[12]

The inner meaning of walking can only be understood when we see it in its entirety. We can walk upright because it is possible for us to develop from creatures woven into the fabric of the world into individual beings confronting the world.

Inherited and acquired movements

As a result of important investigations, Adolf Portmann[13] has pointed out that the first year of human life is of special significance in that the development that takes place in human beings during this period occurs in other mammals within the uterus. Setting this first year apart from the later periods of child development, he calls it the 'extra-uterine spring season'. He says, 'The newborn child can be called a "secondary" nestling because, considering the extent of his development, he is really a fledgling without, however, having acquired a fledgling's free mobility.'[14] The extent of human beings' development at birth indicates their special position in the realm of the living. Portmann somehow divines these inherent evolutionary problems.

Portmann also quotes Fritz Stirnimann's[15] investigations, which must be considered in relation to the findings mentioned earlier concerning the positional and attitudinal reflexes of children. These are known to be spontaneous activities of newborns that occur in response to certain circumstances of stress. Thus, children show that it is possible for them to stand, crawl and walk during the first months. These incipient faculties, however, are lost by the fifth month, thereby making it possible for children to achieve proper crawling, standing and walking only from the ninth month on:

> To be prepared to stand, one must possess the ability
> to place one's limbs in the standing position. To
> demonstrate this in the newborn child different parts of
> the body surface or the eyes must be stimulated. Held
> upright, for example, even the newborn child tends
> to stretch his legs when the soles of his feet come in
> contact with a firm surface. He does not yet show any
> clear readiness to stand, however, but is only capable of
> performing the action when his legs have been brought
> into the proper position. During the second quarter of
> the year, a readiness to stand occurs when the *upper* part
> of the child's foot is touched. When, for example, he is
> held upright so that the upper part of his foot touches the
> lower edge of a table-top, he will bend first one leg and
> then the other. Then, putting the sole of his foot on the
> table, he will straighten his leg out and will finally stand
> with both feet on the table...
>
> It is possible to induce reflex walking movements in all
> normal, healthy newborn babies. To demonstrate this,
> the child is held around the waist with both hands,
> and is stood upright on a firm base. Certain supporting
> reactions in the legs result. If his body is now tilted

slightly forward, he will make proper walking movements and take steps if he is moved in keeping with them. He will have a tendency to cross his legs, but nevertheless steps of about four inches each will be taken. In the course of further development, around the end of the first six months, these walking movements recede into the background and so cannot be said to represent an immediate preparatory step to true walking...

J. Bauer has described something similar as a crawling phenomenon. If one puts a small baby belly-down on a table and supports the soles of his feet with his hands, the baby begins to crawl by pushing himself away from the supporting hands. The arms are lifted and placed forward one after the other, and in this way the child can be made to crawl across the table. According to Bauer, the crawling phenomenon occurs only in the first four months and then only when the child lies on his belly.[16]

In these quotations are characterised the three most important achievements of spontaneous movement in children that occur before they acquire the ability to stand and walk upright. It is of the utmost significance to the proper course of later development that these movements appear during the first months after birth and then disappear, thus making possible their reappearance later in a completely new metamorphosis as crawling, standing and walking.

Without referring to the particular investigations mentioned above, Otto Storch[17] has reported two forms of movement that he calls 'inherited and acquired motor movements' (*Erbmotorik und Erwerbsmotorik*).[18] Although in the case of children one can hardly speak of inherited motor actions being manifested during the first months, congenital movements must nonetheless be differentiated from those acquired by learning, of which walking is the most important.

The findings of Otfried Förster[19] and Cécile and Oskar Vogt[20] are also relevant. They state that premature and occasionally also fully mature babies show movements that may be described as typically athetotic:[21]

> The movements can be described as follows. The arms are bent at the elbows at right angles, the lower arms turned strongly out so that the palms face outwards, while the wrists are stretched or even over-stretched against the lower arms. Simultaneously, these babies play a strange game of stretching, bending and spreading their fingers and toes out by stretching or overstretching them all at once or one after the other.[22]

In the course of the first months these choreatic-athetotic[23] movements pass over into general kicking, which in turn is gradually overcome so that by the end of the first year walking has been learned.

Athetotic children, however, who because of certain brain injuries do not learn to walk or do so only with difficulty, show symptoms that clearly and unequivocally point to the forms of movement just described. Children with the characteristic symptoms of Little's disease show the same *pes equinus* (literally, horse foot) position and the tendency to cross their legs when trying to walk.[24] Thus, in these children, the movements of early childhood described above continue into later life. They present the symptomatology of grave motor disturbances, which cannot be overcome because walking as an acquired motor activity cannot redeem the persisting inherited movements.

Children who cannot develop the reflexes of position and attitude show the crawling phenomena described above. This group, whose disturbances belong to the forms of cerebellar ataxia,[25] remain crawlers throughout life because they cannot acquire the ability to walk upright owing to the failure of their sense of equilibrium.

So-called athetotic children retain the forms of movement associated with premature birth and these then lead to serious disturbances of posture and movement. Here, above all, the directed and ordered movements are disturbed, but the ability to walk upright can still be acquired gradually by quite a few children in this group.

In athetotic children the range of motor disturbances is not a pathological condition that arises anew. These disturbances are rather the physiological remnants of the behaviour patterns of early childhood. The inability to learn to walk upright is common to all of these children because of the retention of early movement patterns that later assume disproportionate dimensions. What has been described earlier in this chapter as the birth of walking out of the chaos of general movement cannot be accomplished by them.

A developmental delay is also shown in the general attitude of these child patients. The lighting up of consciousness that follows the differentiation between self and world (or between body and environment) while walking is being learned, does not take place. Athetotic children struggle to master their feelings and suffer from an erratic, unruly occurrence of laughing and weeping that is beyond their control.

Children suffering from Little's disease are so completely given over to their sense impressions that they cannot control them, or at best do so only with difficulty. A slight noise makes them wince and a strong light intensifies their muscle spasms. This makes any development in space almost impossible for these children, based as it must be on the experience of 'there' and 'here'.

The behaviour of those children who cannot attain positional and attitudinal reflexes also shows that they cannot retain sense impressions. The development of memory occurs only involuntarily, and they are hardly able to consciously call up memories at the right occasion.

From these brief indications it can be seen how fundamentally important walking is for the development of human consciousness and experience. If walking fails to develop, then the control of feelings and moods is missing, the conscious use of the faculty of memory is lacking, and separation of self and world is not achieved. [26]

If we did not learn to walk, further development of the conscious unfolding of the specific human faculties over the course of childhood would not be possible. The way leading to school is in reality open only to those children who can go walking upright. For the others, measures of curative education can compensate for what they have had to forego in the development of the first year even though learning to walk, as an act of grace, could not become manifest in them. [27]

If, in an understanding of the uprightness of human beings, one does not include the observations touched upon here, then the following remark of Portmann can be readily understood: 'The true meaning of the slow development of the completely upright position of the body, and the bodily structure basic to this position, can still hardly be grasped.' [28] Only those, however, cannot grasp it who look at the ability to walk upright as simple locomotion and lack the courage to admit the fundamental difference that exists between the upright position of human beings and that of the higher animals. Endowed as they are with a horizontally oriented spine, the animals remain part of the world. They are overwhelmed by sense impressions and the abyss between self and world does not open up. In them the head is not carried above the spine as if floating, but remains incompletely differentiated as a continuation, not yet a separate creation, at the anterior end of the body.

Memory pictures, therefore, can only be retained, but not recalled. Pleasure and displeasure, greed and disgust, constantly changing, flood their inner experiences. The upright posture alone causes the abyss to open between self and world, and this leads to the further acquisition of speech and thought.

The ability to stand, the reflex walking movements, crawling, and the athetotic movements of premature births differ fundamentally from the new phenomenon of walking. They must disappear in the course of the first year to make walking possible. Whether these archetypal movements are called inherited or congenital, or whether they are attributed to activities of certain nerve centres of the cerebrum or cerebellum, is not as important as to recognise the entirely new impulse brought forth in the acquisition of walking.[29]

From the development of looking and grasping through to the acquisition of walking, a new power unfolds, opposing all biological processes. This force first takes hold of the eyes, brings the axes of sight into line, and thus makes possible the fixation of the gaze. It directs the arms and hands of the body towards purposeful movements, and the hands learn to grasp, to fold and to hold each other. Finally, the soles of the feet touch the ground. From the heels to the toes, they enter the field of gravity – something that does not happen with any animal – and the head is lifted up, reaching into the light. In this picture of the upright position is presented the polarity of light and gravity.

Thus, a new element enters that must be realised as an aspect of human beings that can be attributed only to humans and to no other creature on earth. Rudolf Steiner calls this entity, 'I'. Through their 'I' every human being can receive the gift of grace of walking. When it appears in the form of uprightness, all other forms of movement recede and disappear. It is as if the shepherd enters among the herd, and the herd grows quiet and restful as it gathers around him.

In this way, all other forms of movement arrange themselves around the power of uprightness, which, in the moment it appears, brings order and guidance with it. [30]

The stages of learning to walk upright

Now that we have attempted to approach those phenomena connected with the acquisition of walking upright in a special way, a strange conformity to law is revealed during this period that should be mentioned. It can hardly be mere chance that it takes approximately a year to learn to walk, and that development that is premature or delayed is expressed symptomatically as a disturbance in the unfolding of a child's being. To learn to walk takes the same amount of time as that required by the earth to circle the sun, which suggests that this sun-earth rhythm is inscribed in this human faculty.[31]

Rudolf Steiner has pointed out that we acquire our uprightness here on earth as something entirely new:

> It is significant that we must work on ourselves to
> develop from beings that cannot walk into ones that walk
> upright. We achieve our vertical position, our position of
> equilibrium in space, by ourselves.[32]

This earthly acquisition of the ability to walk is placed in the cosmic-time relationship between sun and earth.

A study of the gradual progress of this year of learning to walk can be expressed as a calendar that has been worked out by a number of observers and shows approximately the following stages:

1st month: Children's eyes begin to fix their gaze.

2nd month: Even when lying belly-down, children begin to hold their heads upright.

3rd month: When placed belly-down, children can lift their shoulders together with their heads and keep them elevated for a time.

4th month: When placed belly-down, they can support themselves on the palms of their hands. They grasp new situations with an active gaze. They begin to reach for objects that they have found by touch. In the act of grasping, children can bring both hands together without using their fingers.

5th month: While lying on their backs, children can lift their heads and shoulders. They have learned to turn from their backs onto their sides, and are also able to grasp with their hands objects they have seen.

6th month: Children are able to sit up with support. They can bring a movable object into contact with a resting one: for example, they can beat rhythmically with a spoon upon a table.

7th month: Children begin to move away from a position of rest. They try to get desired objects and to reach them by changing their position.

8th month: Children now sit independently and begin to crawl.

9th month: Children learn to raise themselves to a sitting position without support. They learn to kneel and begin to stand with support.

10th month: They are able to throw things.

11th month: They can raise themselves and stand by holding on to something.

12th month: Children can stand freely and with a little help and support take their first steps.

If one tries to live imaginatively through this calendar of the first year, then these twelve months appear not only as a schema showing the innate 'intelligence' of the growing baby, but as a year in which the emergence of each acquired faculty is marked by a particular festival.

Rudolf Steiner has said that in earlier epochs of human evolution birth always took place during Christmas time.[33] This remained so up to the third millennium BC, especially among the North Germanic tribes, after which births gradually began to spread out over the whole year. Thus, it was formerly true that children first saw the light of the world at a definite time of the year. Gradually, in the course of the further development of humanity, this link with nature was abolished.

Accordingly, learning to walk in former times was accomplished in the year between one Christmas and the next and, as if into the milestones of incarnations that remained from this, the various festivals were inscribed. These were celebrated first as pre-Christian and later as Christian festivals. While the following correspondences cannot be 'explained' in the ordinary sense, it is left to the individual to try to experience the connections resulting from them.[34]

It may be significant that babies smile for the first time and can lift their heads from the horizontal just at the time when the festival of the presentation in the Temple, Candlemas, is celebrated.

At Easter, babies learn to hold up their heads and shoulders while on their stomachs; they raise themselves above the water so to speak. They reach for objects, answer looks with a smile and touch things. Their arms are freed.

Around Whitsun, they can grasp an object they see and thus coordinate their hands and eyes. They can turn from a back to a side position, freeing themselves from the base on which they lie.

At St John's Tide, children sit up. Now the sun stands at the highest point of the heavens and, as human beings, children hold their heads freely above their horizontal shoulders.

At Michaelmas children sit up by themselves and learn to kneel and to stand by supporting themselves.

At the beginning of Advent, children put themselves freely into space, and by Christmas they can take their first, hesitant steps.

These hints have been given to help those who seek a new understanding of human beings, not to open the gates to mystic speculation. We should practise such thoughts and cultivate the feelings arising from them especially when watching children to whom the ability to walk has been denied. Then a new power to help will call forth the will and bring help where help is otherwise denied. In every child who learns to walk today these words are at work: 'Arise! Take up thy bed and walk!' It is the sun power that raises the earthly body of every individual so that they can walk upright over the earth.[35]

2. Learning Our Native Language

Speech as expression, naming and speaking

Once children are able to raise themselves to an upright position and have acquired free mobility in space, the second step in becoming human follows. They learn to speak and use their native language. This is an especially impressive acquisition and only in recent decades have child psychologists paid deserving attention to its importance. By the time children learn to speak their native language by conquering words and word connections, they have taken a most important step on the path of human development. The tremendous gulf that separates human beings from animals is also indicated here. Portmann is fully justified in saying, 'we must point emphatically to the fact that human speech in word as well as gesture, both of which rest on the principle of communication through signs, is something totally different from all animal sounds.'[1]

Those animal sounds, when made by humans, are also only sound. Cries, screams, moans or other sounds expressing the woes and joys of existence are not speech. Speech[2] is not merely expression, but naming. One of the roots of speech is to be found in the fact that through it *names* are given to the world and its manifestations.

In the First Book of Moses we read:

> So out of the ground the Lord God formed every beast
> of the field, and every bird of the air, and brought them
> to the man to see what he would call them; and whatever
> the man called every living creature, that was its name.
> And the man gave names to all cattle, and to the birds of
> the air, and to every beast of the field; but for the man
> there was not found a helper fit for him. (Gen. 2:19f.)

The giving of names is directly connected with the creation of Eve. With whom, after all, should human beings speak if not with their own kind? They can give names to the animals, and to things and beings. But who is to respond when they begin to speak? The word spoken into space remains without an answer, is shattered and blown away. It dies, and dumbness follows.[3]

These brief remarks hint at the soul qualities that form speech and speaking. Only a small part of speech is an expression of human existence and feeling, and as such it is still intimately connected with human beings' animal nature. When, however, through speech, sounds are raised out of this sphere and the tones humanised, speech then becomes the servant of the word. The sounding tone unites with the power of speech and thus the names of things can be pronounced. It is speech itself working through human beings that calls things by name.

This, however, is not all. Naming is only the statement of fact. Speech strives for something more; it aims at finding a connection with itself. Speech wants to come to terms with the word that is heard in order to understand what it has heard, to answer the question received, to demand answers from out of its own questioning. Therefore, God gives Adam his Eve because only when human beings experience themselves through speech in other human beings do they become aware of themselves.

Speech can now be said to unfold in human beings in a threefold manner:

1. As an expression of what lives in the soul as animality.
2. As an expression of the ability to name all things of this world. Thus, the names of things and beings sound forth.
3. As an expression of the power that tries to meet itself in speaking. Speech thereby gradually comes to terms with itself.

Human beings are connected with this threefold expression of speech through their whole being. At first, however, they are not the one who speaks, but the one through whom speech sounds and expresses itself. For this speech needs its own tools, and these are created in human beings by speech itself.[4] Immature human beings represent an undeveloped natural condition in which speech becomes active in such a way that it is able to become manifest. Even as the artist creates tools from the substances of nature by means of which they fashion their work, so speech takes human beings as the natural substance and creates out of them its own works of art. Thus, human beings ultimately appear as images because through the speech with which they have been endowed, they can become manifest as selves. Human beings can sound through speech (from the Latin *personare*, meaning 'to sound through') as personality and communicate with, or impart themselves to, other human beings.

It was a rather childish agnosticism that imagined, and also tried to prove, that the organs of speech were no more than the larynx with which, when speaking, some small parts of the cerebral cortex are connected, and that these are the essential elements through which human beings begin to prattle. Today we know that it is the whole human being who speaks. As beings of body, soul and spirit, human beings take part in the formation of speech and, in speaking, express themselves as personalities. Rudolf Steiner has described it in the following way:

> What makes us human is our larynx and everything
> that has to do with it … And the rest of the human
> form, down to the smallest detail, has been formed and
> sculpted so that human beings now, at the present stage,
> are as it were a further continuation of their speech
> organs. Our speech organs are, in our present stage, the
> determining factor where our human form is concerned.[5]

What are these instruments of human speech whose further formation and metamorphosis human beings appear to be?

The anatomy of the organs of speech

The larynx, the centre of the organs of speech, is the intricately formed, central part of a pipe through which the breath streams in and out. This pipe, which widens and branches out downwards as well as upwards, is called the trachea or windpipe. Air passes down through the windpipe, then through the two large bronchi that enter the right and left lobes of the lungs. As these tubes penetrate the lungs further, they continue to divide dichotomously, growing smaller and smaller, multiplying over and over again. The final configuration, rightly called the 'bronchial tree', is formed like the trunk of a tree that divides into two main branches. These divide further into smaller ones, finally forming twigs and ever smaller twigs. The only difference between the trunk of this tree and that of an ordinary one is that its roots are in the larynx and its branches grow downwards. Thus, this bronchial tree is upside-down compared to natural trees.

Just as each twig of a tree terminates in a leaf, so each of the numerous bronchioli terminates in an alveolus, a small cell into which the inhaled air streams. There the air meets indirectly the blood that flows around the walls of the alveolus. The inhaled air, changed through this meeting, streams back in exhalation and passes once more through the larynx on its way out. While being breathed out the air gives service to speech. The laryngeal muscles rhythmically move the parts of the larynx, creating a thickening and thinning of the out-streaming air, which forms the pliable basic substance needed for the formation of tone and sound.

The pipe around which the larynx is formed also continues upwards as the pharynx, or throat, which opens into the oral and nasal cavities. From the throat, two small Eustachian tubes lead backwards to the middle ear to connect indirectly with the air vesicles of the temporal bone lying behind.

The mouth, including teeth, lips, tongue, cheeks, and palate, is the sculptor of the sounds of speech. It moulds the air prepared by the larynx to form labial, palatal, dental and lingual sounds, and can cause the prepared air to be aspirated or forced, vibrated or nasalised. From these various combinations the consonants are formed.

The nasal cavity acts as a resonator; it also regulates the amount of air needed.

The Eustachian tubes leading to the middle ear create an intimate connection between speaking and hearing that should not be overlooked.[6]

To arrive at a real and concrete picture of this structure, we would have to say: proceeding downwards, the trunk of the windpipe opens into the two large bronchi. These then continually divide and finally become the numerous air cells, or alveoli, of the lungs. The alveoli, like tender organs of touch, meet the expanding plane of the surrounding blood. So it is that in the lungs the air of the speech organs experiences the touch of the flowing blood. Like so many thousands of little feet, the alveoli touch the surface of the blood, feel its strength or weakness, its speed or hesitancy. They are thus a vastly extended organ of touch that experiences the nature of the blood and reacts accordingly. It is for this reason that we can speak only with great effort when the blood flows too fast and fitfully through bodily over-exertion. Then these organs of touch are swept into the rushing current of the bloodstream and are lost in it. When, on the other hand, the blood flows too slowly, as can happen in some illnesses or in individuals who are sluggish by nature, the connection between these organs of touch and the bloodstream will not be intimate enough and, for lack of strength, speech will be wrested from the chest only with difficulty. Let us keep in mind, therefore, that downwards, below the windpipe, it is the course of the blood that has a determining influence on speech.

Upwards, however, the two Eustachian tubes spread out like arms and with their hand-like ends reach into the vicinity of the ear. There they hold on, grasping the ear so that hearing and speaking, address and rejoinder, can come about in immediate cooperation. In the middle ear the air organism touches the membrane of the eardrum like a hand. The membrane of the so-called circular window, which leads into the mysterious cavity of the inner ear, is also touched. In this way the touching hand of the upper air organism is connected with the inner as well as the outer ear because, while the circular window leads into the cochlea of the ear capsule, the eardrum represents the boundary to the outer acoustic duct.

The mysterious cell where the names of things and beings are hidden is found only in the inner ear. There, the eternal ideas out of which all being and becoming is formed touch the earthly realm of the human organism and pronounce their true names. The air of the speech organism extends up to it like a hand reaching for the word inscribed in all things and beings.

The speech organism reaches above into the region of the ear and thus connects the streaming of the blood with the apprehension of names. It is in this way that the act of hearing comes about for names and words. The air organism exists not only for speaking, but also for hearing, and it intimately entwines both faculties. In the region of the mouth and nose the organs of speech have their workshop where they actively form speech. The speech organism rests on the blood, hears in the ear, and works in the mouth and nose cavities. Its centre, however, is the larynx, balancing above and below like a heart, harmonising and uniting the tendency to fall apart or to collapse upon each other. This is only possible because the larynx is not a rigid tube but a complicated joint that is kept in continual movement by a definite number of muscles. From above and below, from front and back, muscles pass to the larynx, unite with its parts and make it into a distinct organ of the motor system. In this way speaking becomes a motor act for expression.

As already emphasised in the first chapter of this book, every muscle movement calls for the participation of the entire voluntary muscular system and this holds true also for the motor nature of speech. It is completely built into the activity of the whole motor system, is part of it, and cannot function without it.[7]

The German philosopher and sociologist Arnold Gehlen[8] has clearly pointed to this fact:

If, with Karl Bühler,[9] one considers 'representation' as just one of the functions of speech besides expression and communication, one widens the standpoint quite correctly into the sociological, but one still tends to overlook the motor side, which after all also belongs to speech. Regarded from this standpoint, speech utterances are first and foremost movements that can well be transformed into other kinds of movement. These are made use of in the education of the deaf and those unable to speak.[10]

The whole organism of movement is characterised as the necessary foundation of all speech. This in turn presupposes an indirect inclusion of the peripheral and central nervous systems. Thus, the extremely complicated ramification of the whole process of speaking becomes evident. The organs of speech stand like a central formation within the human organism. While they are determined by it, they certainly determine it as well. The air circulated in breathing is their basic substance. It touches the blood below and comes into intimate contact with the ear above. The muscular systems of larynx, throat and mouth, as part of the complete motor apparatus, become the builders of both the substance and the form of speech.

The life of the speech organism begins at the moment of birth. The beginning has been made when the air current is drawn into the body and tone formation is accomplished with the first cry. During the embryonic period, this speech organism was at rest, being built up and formed, but at birth its activity begins, enabling children to gradually learn speech as well as speaking.

Saying, naming, talking – three aspects

Before we describe the successive stages of acquiring speech, a few brief but fundamental explanations of terminology must be made. We pointed out in the first section of this chapter that speech itself desires to come into contact with, and to speak to, itself, that the names of things emanate from speech.[11] Speech gives the names. We should, therefore, assign more importance to speech as a being in itself than is usually done.

We are too easily inclined to say to other people, especially if they are children, 'Think first before you speak.' But who really does this? Do we not often become aware of what we actually mean only after we have spoken? The linguist Otto Jespersen[12] repeatedly referred to the remark of the little girl who said, 'Please let me speak so that I know what I think.' How right this child was! A large part of our speaking is like a conversation we hold with our thinking. But we also converse in this way with others, and it is often this very moment of surprise at our own remarks that gives enchantment to a conversation. [13]

I do not mean to say with this that the expression 'I speak' is not true. I speak, indeed, but by no means do I need to think first in order to say what I mean. In speech the ego as individuality lives not only in the realm of the waking consciousness, where thinking is accomplished, but also in the realm of dream consciousness out of which it speaks.[14]

Even as a movement becomes perceptible only after each of its parts as well as the whole have been completed, so too does speech become fully conscious only after it has been spoken. In most cases it is true that 'I' agree with what I have said, but in cases of mistakes, and especially in pathological conditions, speech becomes a self-existent entity that often, to the horror of the speaker, seems to rise from unknown depths.

'It speaks' and 'I speak' are both true. Speech[15] is an entity independent of me that follows its own modalities and laws, has its own reasoning, is active by itself, and expresses itself in speaking. It dwells within me like the breath that comes and goes. It is an entity that seizes my motor organism and lifts it into the realm of the speech organs, wedding it to the air. It is an entity that also rests on the stream of my blood and reaches up to my ear. It is interwoven with me and yet is something different from what I, myself, am.[16]

I speak the speech. That is the primary given fact, but thereby I express myself – my wishes and feelings, my hidden inclinations, my desires, and my presentiments. All this is contained in the words, 'to say'. I, myself, say what I am by means of speech.

Speech expresses itself in speaking. This is the second function of speaking. Here speech lives in its own realm. It deciphers the eternal and temporal names of things and beings, and in this way I learn to know their names. It is not I who call things by name. In reality, I have been given speech and thus names are revealed to me. I can pronounce and also understand them. All this is contained in the words, 'to name'. Things and beings are named in the realm of speech, and I am allowed to take part in it.

Speech expresses me in speaking. It lets me understand other speakers and turns me towards them. Thus, speech can come to terms with itself and with thinking. Speech is a social structure through which the wall between one 'I' and another 'I' can be bridged, even though often only seemingly. Conversation, talk, exchange of thoughts, all have their home here. This is expressed in the words, 'to talk'. Speech builds the bridges of talking across which I can reach the other 'I'.

What Karl Bühler characterises in a primitive, one-sided way as statement, influence and presentation[17] has its correct application here.[18] Statement is contained in saying, presentation in naming and influence in talking. Speaking encompasses all three, and speech itself is even wider and greater than speaking. Speaking is only the active side of speech,[19] which also has a passive side – hearing. Just as speech can speak, so can it also hear the spoken word, the statement. It can hear itself in me, as well as in others insofar as they are speaking. Therefore, the tool, the speech organism, reaches up into the ear where it participates in hearing.

Thus, speech has two sides: the motor side, speaking, and the sensory side, hearing. Both must work together in unison so that speech itself can become manifest. Speech should be recognised as something comprehensive that embraces these two functions. At the same time, it should also be seen as something self-existent.

Schematically this can be illustrated in the following way:

With this introduction we can go on to consider speech development as such.

The stages of speech development

How the speech organism begins to live at the moment of birth was described in the second section of this chapter. When the first breath of air begins to stream in and out, a child's first cry can sound. With this event the foundation of speech is laid. As definite laws can be observed at work in acquiring the ability to stand and walk upright, so also is the gradual acquisition of speech by young children bound to definite steps as if following a mapped-out plan.

Although the first real words are not spoken before the eleventh or twelfth months, the formation of speech actually begins with the first cry. Stern has pointed out that children approach speaking in a threefold manner. First, through the expressive movements of babbling; second, through meaningless imitation; and third, through meaningful reaction to words addressed to them. These three approaches can be distinctly observed, particularly during the first year. All three, however, are preceded by crying. Babies express sensations of sympathy and antipathy in variations of crying or by making crowing sounds that their mothers gradually learn to understand during the first months.

What is here called babbling in sound formation occurs only at around the third month. Friedrich Kainz[20] says the following about this babbling:

> Babbling is a functional playing of the child with his organs of articulation. Just as kicking exercises the motor apparatus, so does babbling mean an instinctive exercise and use of the muscles of the speech apparatus. It consists in the creation of articulated sound formations of a syllabic and word-like character, which are at first single sounds that finally develop into endless babbling monologues...

> In contrast to the sounds of crying, the products of babbling, without being true sounds of speech, gradually assume the character of speech. This becomes apparent from the fact that, besides vowels, consonants also occur.[21]

This is an apt characterisation of babbling, but it should be emphasised that it never contains word-like but only syllabic formations. All babbling consists of syllables, never of words, and rarely of single sounds. The syllable alone is the living building stone of developing word formation because the word does not consist of sounds. According to Walter Porzing,[22] 'The true members of the word are rather the syllables, and the syllable comes into being through the differentiation of the breath within the stream of sound.'[23]

In babbling, babies gather living building stones for future words. They do so in overflowing abundance and without any sign of rationality. Although speech psychologists have tried to show in the last twenty years that the babbling of babies differs from one nation or culture to another, the results have been disappointing. A French baby no more babbles in French, than does a German baby in German, or a Russian baby in Russian. Over the whole Earth babies babble as if they were preparing themselves for any possible language.[24] As Kainz observes:

> It is almost as if nature, through these many-sided and unspecialised sound productions, wished to create the equipment and disposition for any demands that might arise at a later date and to prepare the child for learning any possible language.[25]

What Kainz expresses here rather professorially can be put more simply as follows. Every baby is a citizen of the world, most certainly not of a country. With the extraordinary manifoldness of the syllables they can form, they have the possibility of learning any possible language. It is also of importance to realise that children born deaf babble to the same degree and extent as those who can hear.[26]

Something more must be added to understand the acquisition of baby talk. The gradual preparation in children for the understanding of everything spoken to them before the end of the first year must also be considered. Although growing babies seem to take in the words and sentences addressed to them with increasing understanding, their comprehension does not yet constitute an understanding of words in its truest sense. Children of this age are given a great number of things to perceive simultaneously, including the sounds of words and sentences. When a mother approaches her son to say a friendly word, when a father bends over his daughter and lets his watch dangle in front of her nose, when an older brother or sister shows their younger sibling a new toy, then the word or the spoken sentence is not of importance to those children, but rather the accompanying gestures and actions, the inner approach.

One should try to feel oneself into babies' way of experiencing. Then one will notice that they do not live in single experiences and relations to single facts, but in the totality and infinite abundance of the gradually unfolding environment. Landscapes of events open up before them with clouds of sensations, with mountains and valleys of movements and gestures, and with pastures and slopes of the feelings of affection towards them. Just as in a landscape the sound of an animal or a human voice may be heard, so babies hear the spoken word as part of the wholeness of their experience. They feel the fullness of their experience as a unity, and the spoken word is not something separate from this. The all-embracing gesture of experience forms a first basis of understanding between children and the world, but the word is still an almost unnoticed part of this totality.

When towards the end of the first year the ability to stand upright occurs, then step by step children and the world grow apart. The landscape of experience begins to disintegrate into distinct parts and children learn to feel themselves separated from the surrounding world. An abyss has opened up between what is without and what is within.

At about this time the babbling baby talk has collected all the syllable building blocks.[27] Speech organs have come into joyful action and children begin to notice that the stirrings and feelings of their own world can somehow find expression in this babbling. They have also been able to acquire from the crumbling landscape of experience definite single features. For example, the words 'tick-tock' begin to be joined with the glittering watch. The sequence of the syllables, 'Ma-ma-ma', are attached not just to the appearance of a child's mother, but also with their longing for their mother and everything that brings comfort, satisfaction and rest.

In this manner the first true speech utterances occur in the thirteenth and fourteenth months, that is, at the beginning of the second year. At first, there was the cry and crying. Then came babbling, though neither of these two sound utterances can be called speaking. Now speaking begins, not by naming things, but rather in such a way that a single word designates a great fullness, a whole landscape of experience in which the individual child, as speaker, has become the centre. The syllable 'Meee' is not only the designation for milk as liquid or food, but it may also mean, 'I want milk', or 'I do not want milk', or perhaps, 'How good the milk is', 'The milk bottle', 'The mother who brings the milk', or even 'The clouds', which sometimes are as white as milk.

This stage, which Stern calls the stage of the one-word sentence, lasts a considerable time, terminating toward the end of the eighteenth month. During this period children acquire between forty and seventy words, which they use as one-word sentences.

According to what has been said in the preceding sections of this chapter, we can call this period that of 'saying'. Children use speech to bring themselves and their strivings to expression by means of one-word sentences. It is not yet speech as such that expresses itself; rather children use speech to report about themselves and their world of experience. They express themselves in speaking.

Just as the sixth month is a decisive turning point in learning to walk when children sit up, so in the sixth month of learning to speak, that is, in the eighteenth month, an equally decisive change occurs. Suddenly and quite spontaneously, children grasp the connection of things through names. They comprehend, often from one day to the next, that each thing has a name. From this moment on their vocabulary increases rapidly so that in the course of the next six months, until about the end of the second year, four to five hundred words will have been acquired. At this time, one often has the impression that the words are raining down. Children catch the single drops and know at once how to handle them, although no one has taught them how to do so.

An immediate understanding for the word itself and its meaning is present. When child psychologists say that children arbitrarily change the meaning of words in this period, they are wrong. Stern points out, for instance, that his nineteen-month-old daughter used the name 'nose' for the toes of shoes: 'At this time, she liked to pull our noses and discovered the same to be possible with the toes of our shoes.'[28] But what more appropriate name than 'nose' could be used? The toes of our shoes are indeed the noses that our feet stretch out from under our skirts and trousers, thus 'smelling' their way through the world.

To the astonishment of her father, this same daughter used the word 'doll' not only for a real doll but also for other toys, such as her stuffed rag dog and rabbit. On the other hand, she did not use the word for a little silver bell that was her favourite toy at the time. Again, nothing need astonish us here because in this child's immediate grasp of names, 'doll' was an image of a person and an animal. Stern's daughter would also use the word 'doll' for pictures of people and animals in a book. The silver bell, however, was something totally different, and the error did not lie with the child but with her psychologist father, who expected the comprehensive concept 'toy' to be recognised by his daughter. For her, however, neither doll nor bell were toys, but among the various forms manifesting in an unfolding world. This can by no means be called a change of meaning in the use of words, but the meaning of words is much more comprehensive and general for children than later on. 'Nose' is simply everything that puts a point out into the world, and 'doll' is everything that is not reality but an image of reality.

For another child, 'Hooh' can be the expression of everything connected with anxiety and surprise: darkness as well as an empty room, a mask or a veil that hides their parent's face, the touch of something too cold or too warm. All this can be 'Hooh'. Because meanings are undifferentiated but immeasurably wide and intimately bound up with the world of eternal ideas, children learn to know that each thing, anything that exists, has a name.

During this time, from the eighteenth to the twenty-fourth months, children live in the realm of speech that is connected with naming. Everything is named, and a tremendous joy fills children during this period in which they feel themselves to be discoverers. Here is the table and there is the window; here is the moon and there are the clouds; mother, father, aunt, Liz, bow-wow – each and everything reveals itself anew through the fact that it is named and can thus be taken into possession. Children are now not only discoverers but also conquerors, because what they can name belongs to them and becomes their property. At this stage, speech awakens to itself and begins to unfold in children's souls. They play with speech and with their words as if the most beautiful golden balls had been thrown to them for them to possess.

During this period not only the number of words grows, but they also begin to be differentiated. Nouns, verbs and adjectives are gradually acquired and experienced according to value and meaning.[29] The following table shows the gradual differentiation of the three categories of words during the second year.[30]

Age in years and months	Nouns	Verbs	Adjectives and other words (except interjections)
1y 3m	100%	–	–
1y 8m	78%	22%	–
1y 11m	63%	23%	14%

This clearly shows that towards the end of their second year children have acquired the building stones for forming the first primitive sentences. The head in the noun, the chest in the adjective and the limbs in the verb form the first basic drawing of the image of the human being as revealed in every simple and complex sentence.[31] Even if the formation of the sentences is at first stiff and rigid, like some jointed doll whose head rests too often on the earth with their limbs stretching out into the air, sentence formation has nevertheless begun. Children have reached a stage in speech development similar to the one they acquired in walking when they could take their first free steps in space. With sentence formation, something has been reached in the realm of speech that was experienced by the motor system in the acquisition of the ability to walk upright.

At first, sentence formation is clumsy. Children are living through the period of naming and therefore the names are jumbled and on top of each other. A boy may say, for instance, 'Fall stool leg Ann John,' meaning 'John fell and bumped his leg on Ann's stool.' The German linguist Georg von der Gabelentz[32] tells of a little girl who, at the age of two, climbed on a chair, fell and was smacked by her mother. She spoke of it by saying, 'Girl stool climb boom Mummy sit-upon bitten' (*Maedi Tul ketter bum mamma puch-puch bissen*). This shows clearly what can be expected in forming sentences during the period of naming. Everything is name, the being as well as the thing, the experience as well as the sensation springing from it.

When the threshold of the second year has been crossed, true sentence formation gradually begins. If previously all words have been names, they now become nouns, verbs, and adjectives. In astonishment, Stern expresses what holds true for this period:

> What effort has to be expended later on at school in learning a second language, which is never really mastered even after many years of practice! On the other hand, the speech of his environment seems to flash upon the normal child of two or three years of age. Without ever learning vocabulary or studying grammar he makes the most astounding progress month after month.[33]

This observation is certainly correct. The occurrence that Stern describes, however, cannot be really understood until one comes to realise that it is not children who learn the language, but the language itself that unfolds within children's speech organisms.

Kainz has the following to say on this matter:

> At first the child becomes aware of the fact that in the number of words at his disposal a great variety is contained – designations for persons and things, happenings and conditions, qualities, actions, etc.[34]

On no account, however, can one say that children become aware of these facts and then make the relevant differentiations. Anyone who has ever observed children at the age of two or two-and-a-half years old knows that such an assumption is nonsense. It is the language that begins to unfold and to express itself in speech, not the individual child. In children the urge arises to tell, and this urge awakens speech, which now reaches the point we called 'talking' in the section above on the three aspects of speech (see page 42). Speech speaks the individual. It hears what sounds from without and surrenders to what the urge of the individual child demands. Their native language is arising.

Our native language unfolds astonishingly quickly in the course of the third year. The sentences, at first so stiff and totally inarticulate, gradually begin to take shape and to assume form and life. Just as when, in the wake of the first steps, the manifold possibilities of upright mobility are acquired only gradually and children must learn through weeks and months of practice to go from walking to running, skipping, jumping, turning and dancing in order truly to conquer space, so also in speaking something similar is happening.

Words begin to develop, to be inflected and changed. A noun is gradually differentiated into singular and plural and transformed by use of the several cases. The verb, as a word designating time, acquires character from the experience of past, present and future. The adjectives begin to indicate comparison, and prepositions and articles come into use.[35] One sees how the shapeless, jointed doll created by the first attempts at sentence formation is imbued with life and soul, how it stretches and expands, and soon begins to walk and skip. Thus 'talking' comes into being.

Only in talking is the true acquisition of our native language accomplished, and this is possible only because children grow up in a speaking environment. Speech speaks with other speakers and expresses the personalities of individual children. It assumes a social character and children grow into a language community, that is, into the community to which they belong.

Babbling babies are citizens of the world. Through the stages of saying, naming and talking – through the acquisition of their native language – they become citizens of their country.[36] Once again they take possession of the world, which at first they had to push away from themselves. It was through the acquisition of uprightness that the separation came about between world and self, but now through the gift of speech the self as person reconquers the world. All that we can name becomes our property, for we learn to possess it when its name is revealed to us.

Children at this age resemble Noah, who gathers around him in the Ark the world that belongs to him. The sons and daughters and all the animals that he himself calls by name, are now his own. Outside is the flood, the waters rise, yet the safety of the Ark gives protection and confidence. That is the situation in which children find themselves when they are about two years old. Soon Noah will release the dove in order to learn whether or not the flood has subsided. Likewise children will send out the doves of their first thoughts as soon as they have acquired the security of speaking.[37]

Learning our native language

Now that the stages of saying, naming and talking in the acquisition of speech have been described, it is easy to see that these three activities are fitted in the most intimate way into what was outlined above in the section on the organs of speech (see page 36). This, though a unit, still shows a threefold form. It reaches below to the region of the lungs where the blood opens itself to the air. Above, it comes in direct contact with the realm of the ear through the Eustachian tubes, and in the centre where the larynx and the organs of the mouth are at work, it surrenders to the in- and out-streaming air. The threefoldness of speech corresponds to this anatomical-physiological threefoldness.

From below, where blood and air meet, and where the motor organism rises, 'saying' ascends. It leads the desires and wishes, the strivings and personal emotions into the realm of speech to give them expression. Here lies hidden a separate world of speech, which uses the one-word sentence far beyond the age of childhood. When we make demands, give orders, or use angry or abusive language, but also when we want something with longing or impatience, it is the sphere of saying that brings this to expression. Whether I yell 'Scoundrel!' to one or 'Waiter!' to another, these are one-word sentences that according to my emphasis express what I mean. Saying breaks forth from below and goes upwards.

From above downwards, however, from the ear to the larynx, 'naming' flows and streams. Where the sphere of hearing becomes the source of a special sense, called by Rudolf Steiner the sense of speech,[38] the names of things have their own world. There speech learns the names and they stream into the region of the larynx and express themselves in speaking. Anything we can name with words has its realm here. Whether they are people or animals, things or plants, concrete or abstract, we grasp them all through names. 'Naming' streams towards 'saying' from above downwards and unites and mixes with it, although it exists in itself. Naming streams down from the ear to the larynx.[39]

'Talking', on the other hand, is born in the streaming in and out of the air in breathing. Therefore, it is the social element in the realm of speech. It weaves between one human being and another, between speaker and speaker. It carries the play of question and answer from soul to soul. Naming streams into us from above, saying mingles with it from below, and thus speaking itself, or talking, appears at the end as if it were a unity. Talking, however, is also an independent element itself and lives in the outward flow of the stream of our breath.

Syllables build the saying. Words form the elements of naming. The sentence becomes the garment of talking. In this way syllables, words and sentences also receive their domain, and here the infinitely complex and manifold ties linking speech and speaking to human beings become apparent. In the previously mentioned lecture on spiritual science and speech, Rudolf Steiner describes the mystery of speech with these words:

> If we want to compare the development of language with anything, we can only compare it with artistic creation. We can no more expect that language copies what it is meant to represent than we can expect that what the artist imitates will correspond to reality. Language only

imitates the outer world as any picture or artist imitates outer reality. We could say that before human beings were ego-conscious beings in the way they are today, an artist was at work in them, as the spirit of language, and our ego has entered a place where previously an artist was at work. This is put rather pictorially, but it expresses a truth. We are looking at a subconscious activity and feel that here we have something which made us, ourselves, into speaking human beings, as works of art.[40]

These words reveal that speech is the work of the spirit of speech, who once created it in human beings. It is a work of art and if we try to comprehend it artistically, we recognise the three members of which we have spoken.

Speech pathology, from stammering to the inability to speak, from word blindness to sensory and motor aphasia, will only be seen in the right way if 'saying', 'naming' and 'talking' are recognised in their specific characteristics. The manifoldness of these conditions can only be understood as the falling apart of this threefoldness, which must become a unity in speaking if speech is to express itself, and as the inharmonious working together of these three members and the inability to weld them together or keep them apart. This is intended merely as an indication because a more detailed treatment of the subject would go beyond the scope of this book.

Whenever one has to deal with speech, its extent, magnitude and dimension seem so vast that it is impossible to do justice to what in truth is an eternal being.[41] Therefore, I will close this chapter with the words that Hamann, the wise man from the north, expressed in his book, *The Last Will and Testament of the Knight of the Rosy Cross*:

Every phenomenon of nature was a word – the sign, symbol and pledge of a new, secret, unspeakable but all the more intimate union, communication and community of design, energies and ideas. All that man in the beginning heard, saw with his eyes, beheld and what he touched with his hands was a living word; for God was the Word. With this Word in mouth and heart the origin of speech was as natural, as near and as easy as child's play.[42]

3. The Awakening of Thinking

Prerequisites for the awakening of thinking

The third year, which we shall now take into consideration, is of decisive importance for the further development of children. In the first year they detached themselves from the world by the acquisition of the ability to walk upright and learned to distinguish between the experience of the surrounding world and their own existence. In the second year, through the birth of speech, the things of the surrounding world were named and the manifoldness of speaking, especially in saying and naming, for the first time brought order into the bewildering diversity of life experience. The outer as well as the inner world could now be threaded on the string of words and primitive sentences. Children take the greatest pleasure in the power of their own words, 'wearing' the speech they have acquired like a festive garment. It gives them a sense of comfort and security. When there's a hole in their garment – if a word or sentence construction is missing or not altogether successful – it can be a source of great disappointment and affect them deep within their soul.

In the third year, the time lasting from the extended acquisition of speech to the appearance of the first period of defiance, an entirely new event occurs: thinking begins to awaken. This happens in quite special moments, often lifted out of everyday life, during which children begin to become conscious of themselves as personalities. These moments may appear only seldom and grow more frequent and decisive only in later years, but during the third year they begin to be seen. Children observe themselves and the world no longer as children but as individuals conscious of their own selves.[1]

Many conditions are necessary for this awakening to occur. Some of these are more important than others, but a diversity of these acquired prerequisites is necessary. I shall mention only the most essential ones that will occupy us further.[2] Firstly, the elaboration of speech must be considered because children begin to learn the correct formation of sentences only at the end of the second year when the word as such becomes a phenomenon that livingly changes and transforms itself. Comparison of adjectives, declension of nouns and tenses of verbs are gradually achieved. In this way the experience of time and space is multiplied and recognition of the things themselves is considerably broadened.

Secondly, the acquisition of memory is an indispensable basis for the awakening of thinking. To this belongs the gradual formation of memories from vague recognition to voluntary reproduction of memory ideas.

A third requirement is play. Here the free activity of children as expressed in ever new forms of play, in the imitation of the grown-up world and the enlivening of their own fantasy, is of fundamental importance. How else would children recognise themselves as individuals if they did not repeat, imitate and, as non-egos, put in front of themselves everything they see happening around them? The true meaning of all play is that it allows children to create the world in such a way that, as creators, they can stand back from what they have created.

A fourth requirement is the gradual comprehension of an idea of time encompassing first the future and later the past. There must also be a gradually developing comprehension of space where one cannot only walk and run, but where individual things are kept, such as toys in the toy box and clothes in the closet. Houses and lanes, fields and paths with their trees and shrubs also become well-known sights. Another thing to consider in understanding certain attitudes of children is that the smaller they are (meaning younger in age) the larger they experience themselves in relation to the world of space.

Finally, we must take note of how percepts are gradually grasped and transformed into ideas, a process intimately connected with the formation of memory, which will be mentioned later.[3]

With all these single soul functions, which in the course of their third year children not only acquire but also develop and connect with each other, we have some notion of the complexity of these developments. What we call the 'awakening of thinking' can only arise in this manifoldness and working together. Speech and ideas, memory and play, the comprehension of space and time are like a circle of kind women bending over the cradle in which a sleeping child is on the point of waking up. Each of these 'kind women' makes a helping gesture and calls an encouraging word to the child. Thus, the process of 'awakening thinking' comes about.

We must next try to describe what this awakening thinking is and what it is not. Only after we have reached an understanding on this point can something be said in clarification of the third year in the life of children.

Human thinking: what it is, and what it is not

First, we must clear away the nonsense of the views that began with Wolfgang Köhler's *The Mentality of Apes*.[4] These views were introduced into child psychology by Karl Bühler[5] and have since spread from his work like a malignant growth (for example, through Heinz Remplein[6]). I refer to Köhler's well-known and instructive experiments on a number of anthropoid apes. Here he tried to show that the results he obtained were primitive achievements of intelligence. For instance, some of the chimpanzees, after unsuccessful attempts, were able to reach fruit that was hung from the ceiling, by piling boxes on top of each other. In another experiment, the 'more intelligent' of the animals learned to put together previously prepared sticks so as to reach fruit lying outside their cage. Several other ingenious methods were used by Köhler to arrive at these so-called achievements of intelligence.

Bühler, as an experimental psychologist, was lured by these experiments into subjecting children eight to sixteen months of age to similar situations. For instance, he put a pane of glass between a child and a biscuit the child wanted in order to test how and when the child would summon the 'intelligence' to reach around the glass for the delicacy. But the child usually failed him. In another experiment, a piece of bread attached to a thread was put in front of a child in such a way that they could reach the thread but not the bread. The child was then supposed to pull the food towards them by means of the thread. The results of these experiments caused Bühler to say in all seriousness:

> Indeed, there is a phase in the life of a child that one
> might well designate the chimpanzee age. In the case of
> this particular child it was about the tenth, eleventh or
> twelfth month.[7]

61

Anyone can accept or reject this as they please. The idea, however, that a ten-month-old child, in the environment of their home, hardly yet able to move, should be compared with grown-up chimpanzees in their cages is possible only with the kind of thinking prevalent at the beginning of the twentieth century. Furthermore, the word intelligence is thoroughly abused here. This animal behaviour – and that is what was meant here – is by no means an achievement of thinking. When placing one box on top of the other, or putting sticks together, the chimpanzees are not intellectually putting two and two together, but their desire for the fruit dictates the movements of their limbs in such a way that they use the objects lying about to satisfy this desire.

It would be an accomplishment of real intelligence only if a chimpanzee would break a branch from a tree and prepare it to use as a fetching stick. Or, again, if it could make a box out of boards by using smaller and harder pieces of wood as nails and a stone as a hammer in order then to put the box to use for a purpose thought out in advance. But nothing of the kind happens in Köhler's experiments in which well-prepared objects are so placed that instinct and desire can make use of them. What happens is nothing more than the bringing together of parts, perceived by the senses, into meaningful order through the power of desire. Nothing like this is meant when we speak here of the awakening of thinking.[8]

Stern once called 'intelligence' that faculty 'which adjusts itself to new demands by orderly disposition of the means of thought.'[9] Stern speaks of 'means of thought' that are the basis for intelligent achievement. These, however, are present neither in chimpanzees nor in one-year-old children, as Köhler or Bühler try to understand them.

The foundations necessary for the awakening of thinking are laid only as speech begins to develop in children.

Speech is like a plough that works the field of the soul so that the seed of future thought achievement can be laid into the open furrows. Even seemingly sensible utterances cannot be interpreted as thought achievement. If, for instance, a child begins to name things and then not only recognises but also designates them upon seeing them repeatedly, this is by no means an act of thought but only of memory within the framework of speech.[10]

Also, when a child begins to identify what they have drawn, painted, or otherwise copied, with the actual object – for example, a picture of a cat – and then calls it by its correct name, even this behaviour cannot be ascribed to the acquisition of thought. While certainly complex, this is almost entirely an act of memory as a function of recognition.

It has already been mentioned that memory, like speech, is necessary for the preparation of thinking. The seeds that are sown into the furrows of the field of speech are those pictures and names, ideas and sensations that memory retains for small children. It is the result of the power of memory that the acquisition of these pictures does not continually dissolve and vanish. Memory alone preserves in children the names of things in their connection with the arising imagery. Out of these seeds grow the first few green blades of true thinking in the course of the third year.

What do we call this thinking? In their third year, for example, children have great difficulties in acquiring an idea of space or time. They can ask, 'Is today tomorrow?' or, 'Is yesterday today?' Stern tells how one of his children said, 'When we travel home, it is today.' Or again, 'We want to pack today and travel yesterday.' Something here endeavours to bring into a correct order yesterday, today and tomorrow so that something that exists, though not perceptible, touchable or audible, still receives its rightful place. Children already know intuitively that there is a 'has been' and a 'to come'; it lives in them as a dim feeling. That 'today' may become tomorrow's 'yesterday', however, emerges only gradually as a thought structure from the experience of manifold world happenings. It is these invisible but thinkable structures, inscribed into the experienced reality, that children begin to grasp.

If, one day, a child begins to ponder during a meal and says, 'Daddy spoon, Mummy spoon, Auntie spoon, Bobby spoon, all spoon!' they have made the truly tremendous discovery that there are objects of the same order. They have come to know that not every single thing has its own name, but a number of the same things have a common name, that all spoons are called 'spoon' and that everybody – Daddy, Mummy, Auntie and themselves – possesses a spoon. The great moment has come when thinking begins to awaken to a conscious function. The first acts of thinking do not occur before this time, but after this they continue to increase as children grow older, until at school age they become regular, daily activities.

We should not, as still happens today, mistake purposeful soul activities that will lead to ordered actions for true acts of thinking. Even the unconscious accomplishes many of the actions it quite reasonably strives for. Animals often show in their behaviour unimaginably clear and concrete reasoning. Indeed, reasonable behaviour is evident in the way bees build their combs, ants prepare their food, wasps safeguard the future of their brood. Hundreds of such examples could be given. This kind of reasoning, however, works out of the organic realm and does not comprehend itself. As active intelligence it only uses organisms as tools.

In contrast, the thinking of children, when it awakens in the third year, is reason that comprehends and becomes conscious of itself. That power lying hidden in all things, which orders, works and shapes, now arises in the human head as body-free activity and grows into awakening thought.[11] This even occurs for the first time in the course of the third year. It will occupy us in detail in later sections of this chapter. First, however, the pre-requisites that lead to the activity of thinking must be studied.

Speech as the first prerequisite for thought

After children have learned 'saying' and 'naming' in the course of their second year and have tried to express themselves in somewhat wooden sentence fragments, the whole realm of speech begins to quicken in the third year. As we have already mentioned, we can actually experience how the helpless jointed doll of the first attempts at sentences is gradually permeated with life and soul, how it stretches and expands and soon begins to walk and to hop.

What children now acquire is the living incorporation of what they later have to learn intellectually as grammar.[12] Especially the morphology of words and the art of forming sentences, or syntax, begins to awaken in children. Language gives birth to itself in all its perfect grandeur and beauty. Now declination, conjugation and comparison are learned, not in the way they will be learned later, however, but in such a way that, through children's imitation and agility, the words themselves unfold their own life. The endless possibilities of description for everything offered children by the variety of their experiences thus arise. Merely in the fact that they begin to use nouns, verbs and adjectives, the world opens up to them as being in existence (noun), is constantly active in doing and suffering (verb), and is also subject to judgment and description by others (adjective). Thus noun, verb, and adjective form the archetypal picture not only of all sentence formation, but of all manner of manifestations of earth existence.

With the beginning of the declension of nouns[13] comes children's first sensations for the way things and beings appear and are related to each other: in the nominative still isolated, limited and related to itself; in the genitive describing ownership, membership, partnership; in the dative referring to the quality, the place, the time and grasping the thing or being as object; and in the accusative describing more the quantity, representing the spatial expanse and the length of time.[14]

The differentiation between singular and plural, between masculine, feminine and neuter begins to emerge. Something like the theory of categories as they were first discovered and described by Aristotle comes alive.[15] In speaking, children repeat on the level of the word all relations of things and beings of the surrounding world. When even the verb with its conjugations gradually becomes their property – as transitive, intransitive or reflexive, indicating whether it is a case of general activity (to blossom, to think, to fall) or relating to a person or thing – then a feeling for the manifoldness of all that happens arises in children. When through conjunctions the activity of the event is so described that it can be represented according to person, number, time, manner and condition, the application of this theory of categories is extended almost without limit.

When children begin to speak about past and future, concepts of time are evolved that lead later to a past perfect and imperfect or conditional, and to a picture of the conditional. They gradually learn to define themselves as subjects acting in the present.

With the adjective, children learn to point to single characteristics and to ascribe to a thing consisting of many relations and qualities one definite characteristic that singles it out. These single indications are also discovered in other things and compared with the quality comprehended first. In this way comparison is gradually developed. That this does not come about easily is demonstrated by the study of a child called Annie, who, when shown the drawings of three towers of unequal size at the age of two-and-a-half years, said that one of them was large, the other small and the middle one thick.[16] The comprehension of a comparable ratio of size did not yet exist. For some time, this comparison seemed to Annie the only possible one because the comprehension of the comparison of three similar things is only formed towards the end of the third year.

An endless number of examples could be cited to demonstrate gradual maturing in the comprehension of a living grammar. Children are also much more mobile than adults in declension and conjugation, and use words with an overflow of formative power. A child will not say, 'The sheep,' but 'The sheeps,'; not, 'The feet,' but, 'The foots,' in order to mark the difference between singular and plural in the form of the word.[17]

But these are all only a preparation for thinking, not yet the act of thinking itself. They are the numberless furrows and figures that the plough of speech imprints into the field of the soul. Rudolf Steiner once pointed out the fundamental difference between thought and speech when he said:

> Human thinking takes place to a large extent consciously.
> Speech is not conscious in the same degree. A person
> needs little self-consciousness to realise that they do not
> speak with the same degree of consciousness with which
> they think.[18]

In this half-consciousness, which does not lie as deep as dream consciousness, but unfolds in the region between dreaming and waking, children learn to speak.

When children produce new designations for things they cannot yet name, when they produce names that are either entirely new creations or combinations or transformations of otherwise known words, it is not a result of their own thinking, but rather the innate formative force of language that performs this and expresses itself through them. When, therefore, Annie was asked the name of her clown (Punch), she first said, 'Rinka', then 'Rinkus', then 'Pasta'. She produced a kind of word salad in her joy of creating new words. Elsa Köhler[19] observed correctly when she added, 'I believe Annie would be able when in full swing, to improvise another half dozen new words.'[20] The same child called skimmed milk 'water-milk', a rubble heap 'dirt mountain', a mortar 'sugar rammer' or 'sugar stamper', and the railway conductor 'Mr Railway Station', explaining, 'the man in the train … who pinches the cards.' But this is not the case of an explanation of a thought-like nature, but a description and combination of sense and speech experience.

These examples show the tremendous plastic power that lives in the language of children. This calls to mind an indication of Rudolf Steiner's:

> People before the Fall could not have spoken in the way
> we do now, because speech had not been differentiated
> into different languages; for this differentiation depended
> on a quality of permanence entering speech … Instead of
> there being a language with the quality of permanence,
> each thing, each impression would immediately be
> answered by a sound from within. The word would
> be wholly at one with the outward reality. What has
> developed in the form of speech or language is but the
> earthly projection, the fallen or residual nature of this
> living, fluid language.[21]

A trace of this originally intended state reappears in the ever-recurring new word creations of children.

Through the totality of grammar, the 'fallen or residual nature' of language carries within it as image the reasoning of the whole universe. Of this Steiner speaks at length and shows how living forces of reason permeate single words, so that the French word 'courage', for instance, combines the words 'coeur' and 'rage' and thus points to the life and enthusiasm radiating from the heart. That is how reason would describe the word 'courage'. According to Steiner, 'These are not arbitrary inventions but actual phenomena. It is in this way that words are formed.'[22]

We now come to the first understanding of that mighty foundation that the world of speech gives to children for the development of their thinking. In the realm of speech as a whole, there lives an all-wielding reason in which children take part when they speak. They cannot yet think alone and independently, but, in speaking, they practise the rules of reason, for grammar is the logic of language, a universal logic that later will be raised to the individual logic of the thinking person.

Memory

The second sphere into which children grow in their third year is the realm of remembering and memory. In the course of the third year the development of the faculty of memory receives a decisive impetus and assumes its rightful place. At the end of the third year, memory has been so far perfected that it has become a fundamental part of the experience of consciousness. From this time on the thread of memories develops and soon becomes a continuum for daily experiences.

Though this development of memory is of great importance for the awakening of thought, these two soul activities are fundamentally different. The development of memory in small children poses many problems.[23] In basic outline, however, the development of memory is open to study nowadays, especially on the basis of what Rudolf Steiner has to say. He once described how, in the development of human history, a threefold transformation of the faculty of memory has taken place. In primeval times of Atlantean development[24] it began with the formation of a localised memory:[25]

> If in that time of which I have spoken one were to enter the region inhabited by people who were still conscious of their head, chest, heart and limbs, one would see on every hand small pegs placed in the earth and marked with a sign. Or here and there a sign made upon a wall. Such memorials were to be found scattered over all inhabited regions. Wherever anything happened, a person would set up some kind of memorial, and when they came back to the place, they lived through the event over again in the memorial they had made.[26]

This localised memory was followed by rhythmical memory:[27]

> Human beings felt a need so to reproduce within themselves what they heard that a rhythm was formed. If their experience of a cow, for instance, suggested 'moo', they did not simply call her 'moo', but 'moo-moo' – perhaps, in very ancient times, 'moo-moo-moo'. That is to say, the perception was as it were piled up in repetition, so as to produce a rhythm.[28]

Rudolf Steiner calls the third form of memory, 'time memory':[29]

> Only in the third stage does that develop which we still
> know today – *temporal memory*, when we no longer have
> a point in space to which memory attaches, nor are any
> longer dependent on rhythm, but when that which is
> inserted into the course of time can be evoked again later.
> This quite abstract memory of ours is the third stage in
> the evolution of memory.[30]

At the transition from the Atlantean to the post-Atlantean
epoch around the year 8000 BC, the change from localised
to rhythmical memory took place. When the high cultures
of Asia Minor were succeeded by that of Greece, at about
the time of the Trojan War and the laying of the foundation
stone of Europe, rhythmical memory changed into picture
or time memory.

It is quite obvious that localised memory is established
through our limbs by erecting markers in our surroundings.
Our hands build primitive and simple memorials.
Rhythmical memory utilises the element of speech and
song. Finally, picture or time memory pertains to the head.
Accordingly, these three forms of memory ascend and
wander from the movement of the limbs up to the resting
head via the motor activity of speech.[31]

It is significant that there still exist in the German
language words exactly indicating these memory forms.
There is the word *merken* (to remember), which we still
have in *Marke, Markierung, Markstein* (mark, marking,
landmark). I mark something in the sense of 'mark my
word' by making a remark about it to myself or finding
a landmark outside for it. The second word is *besinnen*,
which comes from *sinnen* (to meditate, ponder, think, to
be minded). The sound already contains a rhythmical
element, which may turn from the inward *sinnen* to the
outward singing. Songs and sagas, those rhythmically
recited epics that call up in the listener the rhythmical

memory, belong here. From the *Bhagavad Gita* to the Songs of Homer and the *Nibelungenlied,* they formed and fashioned rhythmical memory. The third word is *Erinnern* (re-member, re-collect). What was laid into the innermost soul now reascends as *Er-innerung* (re-collection).[32] This is the form of memory that prevails today and that we all know.

Thus, we can draw up the following table to indicate the totality of memory.

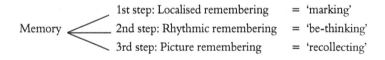

	1st step: Localised remembering	= 'marking'
Memory	2nd step: Rhythmic remembering	= 'be-thinking'
	3rd step: Picture remembering	= 'recollecting'

These stages of memory are strikingly featured in the development of children's memory. Karl Bühler has an inkling of this when he says:

> It is a fact that what we differentiated abstractly as a path from below upwards through steps or phases, the child passes through in the development of his memory activity in all reality. This means that we can discover first vague impressions of familiarity ... then the experiences of more definite recognition and finally complete memories ordered according to space, time and logic.[33]

Bühler describes indistinctly what appears clearly in the threefoldness of memory as outlined by Rudolf Steiner.

During their first year children are filled almost entirely with a localised memory. They experience the impressions of familiarity, described by Bühler, when the faces of their parents appear again and again, when older siblings bend over the side of the crib, when light and darkness alternate. Here 'landmarks' appear from outside and vaguely fashion the basis of 'marking' (*merken*).

In the second year, when speech develops, rhythmic memory begins to be formed. Newly learned words are now said over and over again to exhaustion, and new forms of movement are continually repeated. A picture book is repeatedly brought out and looked at as the acquired sounds are uttered. During their second year children seem possessed by rhythm and repeat everything they do. Moreover, localised memory expands. Certain places are sought out with pleasure, others avoided with trepidation because certain memories are connected with them. At the same time the beginnings of the third form of memory appear. As Stern describes it:

> These first traces of memory ideas (*Erinnerungsvorstellungen*),
> even if only fleeting, appear from the second year
> onward. Around the middle of the second year,
> however, memories of longer duration also begin
> to emerge. Here the twenty-four hour period has a
> preferential position (in the order of periodicity).[34]

He is justified in pointing to the periodicity because the picture memories are still shadows over against the lively experiences of the rhythmic memories.

When a two-year-old child demands that the same thing should happen every day at the same time, or that a fairy tale must be repeated with the same expressions and accents of feeling, it is indicative of the rhythmic memory that governs this age.

Towards the end of the third year, memory ideas become more frequent and insert themselves widely into the totality of memories. The ability to 'mark' (*Merkfähigkeit*) and 'be-think' (*Besinnung*) are gradually overpowered by the third form of memory.

Children now learn to remember what has been

73

imparted by means of speech and they become receptive to teaching and admonition. These acquisitions are already the result of the awakening thinking. More will be said about this later.

Around this time children acquire the first picture of their past as the power of reflection begins to unfold within them. Stern describes it in an impressive way:

> We have already had to emphasise in several places the slight acquaintance between the little child and his past. It is true that he owes all his knowledge and his capabilities to his past and its after-effects, but he is not yet able to look back to it … In the mist that hides the child's past from his consciousness, faint, indistinct and fleeting points of light appear here and there. They grow plainer, more varied and frequent with increasing years, and later combine in somewhat greater numbers … Many years pass, however, before these separate parts unite and form a whole, giving the child a connected picture.[35]

In this way, towards the end of the third year, the memory frame for the experience of personality is formed. As an awareness of the past gradually begins to emerge, children are now far enough along to gain an idea of their personalities. This is at first only a dull sensation, but in contrast to the situation of smaller children, it exists. Closed forms of children's existence light up within them only in their recognition of things and situations, or in the rhythmic repetition of actions including speaking.

Thus, the acquisition of memory becomes one of the most important prerequisites for children's experience of their own selves.[36]

Fantasy and play

In connection with the appearance of picture memory, which is in effect a result of the forming of ideas, another soul power, fantasy, grows in children. Rudolf Steiner has shown the polarity that exists between memory and fantasy or imagination:

> Just as pictorial thinking is based upon antipathy, willing is based upon sympathy. If sympathy is strong enough, as when thoughts become memory through antipathy, then imagination is created through sympathy.[37]

Presented schematically these connections can be seen more distinctly:

Knowledge:	Will:
Antipathy	Sympathy
Memory	Fantasy

Stern, at the beginning of his chapter on play and fantasy, indicated the significance of fantasy when he wrote: 'Where shall we begin and where end? The material available is nowhere so overwhelming as in the consideration of fantasy and play.'[38] Fantasy is one of the strongest characteristics of infancy, but it also has a special position that is not always clearly recognised. One is too readily inclined to derive the power of fantasy from the ordinary life of ideas of children. Even Stern does not get beyond this prejudice:

> The concrete image of the fantasy-percept is not, however, the direct production of outer impressions, but the result of inner working ... The percept (*Vorstellung*) is experienced independently and enjoyed as the child's own creation.[39]

One does not attain a true view of those forces underlying fantasy with this interpretation because fantasy takes hold of any kind of material, movements as well as ideas, for activating itself. Any of these materials is the plastic substance used by fantasy. When a child grasps a stick and makes out of it a horse, a hat, an arrow and then a doll in quick succession, what they have done has little to do with the stick itself. Or if, when prompted by an idea, they make themselves into a soldier, a father or a mother, or a conductor, this action also has little in common with the idea. Fantasy seizes anything it can get hold of. Only by recognising the intimate interweaving between play and fantasy can we do justice to fantasy, because fantasy without play is just as unthinkable as play without fantasy. Even when children begin to make up stories at bedtime, this, too, is play, a play of fantasy with the ideas of memory.[40]

Here we have two pairs of contrasts that we must consider. Just as fantasy is bound up with playing, so does memory work in close union with speaking. The faculty of memory is most intimately connected with the faculty of naming because one truly remembers only what is to be named. The memory picture in turn is developed with the name. Play, on the other hand, enlivens fantasy; conversely, fantasy kindles and diversifies play.

When Stern says, 'Fantasy is never able to create out of nothing. Its elements must always have their foundation in real experiences,'[41] one has to reply that in reality it seems to be exactly the other way around. Real experiences have their sources only in children's fantasy. After all, children can grasp their environment only as an interpretation of their fantasy, and existence gains its true meaning and becomes experience in this way alone. Fantasy is the continuous joy that children experience on waking to the earthly world. Their inclinations towards all things and beings, their joyful urges to take everything in, to connect things with each other, to mix and to enhance, is fantasy, and its expression is play.[42]

Memory on the other hand is the result of children's painful collision with the world. The experience of the surrounding world as something alien, something veiled and impenetrable, gives children the power of memory. In memory they can abstract the world, a process similar to what happens in the formation of words, and the world thereby becomes property, albeit a painful and abstract property.

When we see a foal jump in the meadow, we directly experience the fanciful (fantasy-filled) play of the animal. It is pleased with itself in the joy of existence, in the happiness of being part of the world. Its power of fantasy makes it skip and gallop, neigh and shake, and what is so charmingly revealed here for such a short span of time in animals, becomes apparent in children over many years and in manifold ways. The continuous joy of existence and uniting ever anew with the surrounding world, this dawning and all-embracing sympathy is the origin of all fantasy.[43]

Like all play, fantasy, too, has its well-spring in motor activity. Small children take their fantasy from movement and mobility, from their ceaseless need for lively activity. When children move their arms, each movement becomes a corresponding picture. When they run or skip, jump or climb, immediately and naturally each of these forms of movement is embedded in a story that often begins or ends in fragments – it begins without ending and ends without having begun. But that is the fascination of all play, that there is no beginning and no ending, and yet all is happening.

Only later, when movement is performed without a picture behind it, when movement is done for movement's sake, when it has become purpose in itself, will the abstraction of sport be attained.

When, towards the end of the second year, motor activity has freed itself, fantasy begins to arise and gradually take form in the course of the third year. From then on it is preserved during most of childhood and is forced down into the subconscious just before puberty by a thinking that forms ideas and memories that advance with ever-increasing strength into the foreground.

One of the first to do justice to fantasy was Ernst Feuchtersleben.[44] He devoted a whole chapter to it in his *Diaetetik der Seele*, where he said:

> Fantasy is the bread winner, the prime mover of all single members of the spiritual organism. Without it all ideas stagnate, however great their number. Concepts remain rigid and dead, sensations raw and sensuous ... One can say fantasy is in us before we ourselves are, and it remains until we have gone.[45]

These words point to the all-embracing power of fantasy, which beyond childhood comes into the foreground of the soul only when it is withdrawn from waking consciousness and is enwrapped in the dreams of narcotic confusion of memory and thought.

So we see in the third year a period during which children make a threefold acquisition. With the powers of the head, they gradually come into possession of memory in the form of ideas. With their middle organisation they gain speech, learn to form sentences, and begin to hold real conversations: talking is acquired. Finally, fantasy, born out of the limb system, comes to full blossom. This threefold acquisition is the necessary preparatory step for the beginning of the activity of thinking proper in its first tender form. The highest gift bestowed upon us as growing human beings – our cognition, our ability to know – is developed in the soul realm of remembering, speaking, and fantasy. In this process of the awakening of thought, children become conscious of themselves and the word 'I', as self-designation, is used at the same time. 'I think' becomes at first a rare experience whose recurrence gradually increases.

The earliest achievements in thinking

Elsa Köhler describes Annie's first attempts at thinking at the age of two years and six months in the following way:

> When there is something that Annie does not fully understand, she ponders, stands quietly and puts her hands behind her back; her eyes grow large and gaze into the distance; her mouth contracts a little and she is silent; after this exertion she gets a little tired; the expression vanishes; nature arranges for relaxation.[46]

Awakening thought reveals itself here in its outer gesture. Children withdraw from the world of sense impressions, overcoming the impulse to move, and assume a position similar to that of listening. They begin to listen to their awakening thoughts.

These first, softly sounding thoughts contain the dawn of an understanding that the world of things and beings show mysterious relationships; that here and there, at different places, the same thing can happen and that tomorrow and today similar events can take place; that definite objects perform functions appropriate to them and that every human being stands in similar connections to other human beings.

Thus, Annie had learned in her second year to call her father 'Daddy' and all other men 'Uncle'. Before that, all men had been Daddy, her Daddy. But at the end of the third year when she saw a young man leading a dog, she said, 'Look, the dog goes for a walk with his Daddy.' She had grasped the connection 'child–father', and this was shown soon afterwards when she called an uncle with whose son she was playing, 'The other Daddy.'

At about the same time Annie played a question game with her father. In answer to the question, 'Who makes the dress?' he said, 'The dressmaker.' Annie persevered and then asked, 'Who makes the apron?' At the same moment she remembered that the apron she was wearing was sewn by her mother. The father, who knew nothing of this, answered, 'The dressmaker.' Annie, however, interrupted him and said, 'No, Mummy! Mummy is a dressmaker.' With this Annie had discovered an activity that was not only that of the dressmaker, but also that of her mother. The result was the identification of an activity, and her world had become richer by a new connection.

Such identifications start in the course of the third year and are at first simple, becoming more complicated and manifold later on. The same Annie at the age of two years and five months was given a doll named Tony. One day her aunt drew a picture of Tony on a piece of paper. Annie got quite excited because she recognised her doll and yet sensed that the drawing was something different from the object itself. After she had then found and brought Tony to her aunt, she was asked about the meaning of the drawing. She explained, 'A dolly… like that!' The moment this is grasped, the tension dissolves. Object and image are recognised!

By means of speech, children find their first access to another achievement in thought that, along with identification, is of the greatest importance: the relationship expressed by 'when … then', 'because', or 'for' – the fact that one thing happens when or because another thing happens. The first primitive formation of subordinate clauses help children take a big step forwards. Stern calls this the fourth speech stage, he says:

> Like inflexion, hypotaxis (the subordination of one
> sentence to another) is a form of speech completely
> wanting in many languages that can express the
> dependency relationship of thoughts only by putting
> sentences side by side (parataxis).[47] The child of a
> European civilisation passes this stage in about two and
> a half years and proves that he has grasped not only
> the logical connection of thoughts but also their value
> relationship as represented in principal and subordinate
> clauses.[48]

Stern's daughter, Hilde, could already manage the following formulation of sentences at the end of her third year: 'That moves that way today because it is broken'; 'You won't get a sandwich because you are naughty'; 'Must take the beds away so I can get out'; 'Dolly disturbed me so I couldn't sleep.' Innumerable relations of space, time, causes and essentialities are grasped here. What, at the beginning of the third year, still lay in dusky twilight and began to brighten only through single points of light, is plunged into clear light. It has become apparent that the things of the world are connected with each other through manifold relations. The categories of Aristotle are revealed to children as a basis for their achievements in thought.

In children's third year it really is as if the sun of thinking has appeared above the horizon and brightly illuminated the relations that have been formed between all their experiences. They enter the awakening day of their developing life. Not only objects, but also activities and attributes are included in these relations. Thus Annie, who was a city child and saw canned peas in a shop, comprehended the connection, 'Peas grow in cans, and beans grow in glass,' because she had seen the latter at home preserved in glass jars. Where else should they grow? Four weeks later (at two years and seven months) she was shown a picture of flowers in a meadow and said, 'Little flowers in the meadow … grow there!'

Köhler, full of the impressions gained from observing Annie, writes:

> With the collection of concepts, indeed, in the very midst of the labour of collecting, productive thinking grows from now on through its own law that must determine from within the spiritual development. Threads weave to and fro, everything is related, levelled, separated, discarded, wherever necessary. Judgments lie quite open within reach, even where formulations in speech cannot yet follow.[49]

Thinking even overtakes speech. It runs ahead of it, and speech formulations themselves already come partly under the power of children's own thoughts. It is no longer speech alone that utters the words, but children's experiences in thought begin to make use of speech. Movement and speech, which so far have followed rather autocratically their own laws, come under the rulership of contemplation and judgment. Step by step thought becomes ruler of the soul, whose functions bow down under its light-filled majesty.

That is also the radical difference that exists between walking and speaking, on the one hand, and thinking on the other. Walking and speaking are learned; they unfold step by step and give children sureness of movement in space and of behaviour in the world of things and beings. Walking enables children to dominate space and speaking to possess the named world around them. Thinking on the other hand, as a power of the soul, does not use a manifest bodily tool. It uses neither the limbs, nor the speech organs; it appears like a light, which must have been in existence even though it was not visible before. If we should assume it to be created anew in each child, we would be like those who imagine the sun to be a star newly created every morning.

Thinking fills the being of children from the beginning. It is in existence and at work but has no possibility as yet to show itself. It dwells in the distant depths of children's existence, which in the first two years is occupied with the proximity of the body, its sense perceptions, its sensations and feelings. A thorny hedge, behind which thinking is still asleep in the castle of the head, grows out of the manifoldness of these first experiences. It can only occasionally, but sometimes even in earliest babyhood, wake up and appear almost tangibly, though making no utterance. That happens when the dream-sleep existence of early childhood is interrupted by a painful illness. Then the eyes of the baby wake up and become the deeply serious messengers of its individuality. I have often been able to observe this myself. A mother whose child was operated on at the age of six months, described it once to me as follows: 'She is quiet and peaceful, still serious, but really removed beyond her age – yet entirely human. The baby has almost receded into the background. One must observe this only with respect and love.' Once illness has passed, the infant re-emerges and thinking withdraws until it appears in the course of the third year and begins to perform its activities with the help of speech, memory and fantasy.

Like the sleeping beauty it is then kissed awake by its prince. This is a phenomenon that occurs in every child during their third year and one that belongs to the most mysterious events in the realm of the human soul. The individualities of growing children break through the thorny hedge of their daily experiences and awakens their slumbering thinking. In that moment when they behold one another face to face, the consciousness of the individual ego first awakens. This special instant, of which some grown-ups still have a memory, is a turning point in human life. From this moment on an unbroken memory thread exists that carries the continuity of the ego-consciousness.[50] Even if much of it is forgotten in later years, a dim feeling of the unity of our own person extending back to this point in time remains. Behind it, early childhood lies veiled in darkness.

In his autobiography the publisher and writer Karl Rauch[51] describes this special moment in a captivating way:

> I have a distinct early memory picture of a spring day. I may have been three years old, a child among children. The sun was shining, it was late forenoon. Some cousins were with us on a visit. It must have been one of the many children's birthdays in the family. We were romping about among the flower beds and then ran over a wide piece of ground that was waiting to be dug, right across the garden to a ditch in which the first green grasses and herbs were sprouting, while in between the brownish pink Pestilence Wort grew exuberantly. I still know distinctly how I was running, can clearly see my older sister running in front of me as the leader of the whole host of children who raced ahead, and I feel quite consciously when I look back today of how I suddenly stopped running, looked behind me and recognised again at some distance behind me the dozen or so other children, all racing and running. Just as I turned forwards again in the direction of my sister and the ditch, it came over me, that first consciousness, breaking through as clear as spirit, of my own self with this thought flashing up, 'I am I, I – there in front my sister, there behind the others, but here I, myself, I.' And then the race went on.

3. THE AWAKENING OF THINKING

I reached my sister, grabbed her quickly by the arm while running and overtook her. Immediately afterwards all was again submerged, engulfed by the turmoil of the throng of children at play.[52]

Immediately, suddenly and unforeseen, this flash of recognition hit Rauch's soul in the midst of a wild game and, from then on, the consciousness of his own personality remained.

Moriz Carrière[53] described the same phenomenon in the following way:

That I differentiated myself from the world, confronted the external things and grasped myself as self, occurred later (after the second year); I stood in the yard on the street; I could still today show the spot. I was a little surprised at this event, or rather at this deed.[54]

The German author Jean Paul[55] has described this moment perhaps most beautifully:

Never will I forget the phenomenon, never told to anybody, when I stood at the birth of the consciousness of my self, of which I can tell place and time. One morning I stood as a very young child at the front door and looked left toward a pile of firewood when, suddenly, the inner vision, 'I am an I', struck down in front of me like a flash of lightning from heaven and radiantly remained ever since. There my 'I' had seen itself for the first time and forever. Deceptions of memory can here hardly be thought of, as no tale of strangers could be mixed up with what happened nowhere else but behind the veils of the holiest of holies of the human soul, the newness of which has given permanence to such everyday circumstances.[56]

The poet fully comprehends and recognises this event that occurs 'in the holiest of holies of the human soul', where the bride of cognition is awakened by the king's son of the individuality. From this moment onward both are united and remain so until death.

At the awakening of thinking something becomes apparent that is not so obvious in the case of walking and speaking, namely, that all three faculties have metamorphosed out of pre-earthly activities in order to appear in children as in earthly garments. Rudolf Steiner gave concrete indications of this. During embryonic life these three high human faculties are forming a chrysalis in order to emerge step by step after birth. Prior to conception, during pre-natal life, walking, speaking and thinking were three spiritual faculties given to human beings in their purely spiritual existence.[57]

The sleeping thinking awakens at the call of the personality that finds itself. Whoever remembers this moment sees in full detail the circumstances then prevailing. Everything down to the last detail is remembered because the impression is so strong and lasting that no part of it can be forgotten.

From this point on, children speak of themselves with full consciousness as 'I' because they feel that this word is no longer a name but 'the name of names'. Everything that has a name has also somewhere an 'I'. Human beings, however, can know this and express this knowledge; they name themselves no longer as a thing or a being, but as that innermost part of all being and existence, which in their awakening thinking they have learned to comprehend as 'I'.

The first defiance, and birth of the lower ego

Towards the end of the third year when walking, speaking and thinking have been acquired in their fundamental structures, the first phase of childhood development closes and something entirely new takes its place. Children grow into the first age of defiance.[58] The German psychologist Adolf Busemann[59] characterises it as a phase of excitation because feeling and will, working together as affect, step into the foreground and determine children's behaviour.[60]

The ego feeling also increases and with it, defence and rejection in the form of defiance repeatedly break through. Suddenly children no longer want to be led. They withdraw their hand from that of the grown-up and stomp off alone. They want to dress and undress by themselves and often refuse to join in and play with other children, becoming for a time a 'lone wolf'. Conflicts with the surrounding world pile up and parents and educators, without insight and understanding, exercise authority and punishment where help and example, gentle guidance and intuitive forgiveness would be the only right attitude. Köhler, from her experience with Annie, aptly describes this:

> The child is something new to herself. What is feeling
> and willing in her is something new to her, from
> which thinking has not yet gained any distance. Thus,
> a tremendous contest goes on within her. Once the
> breakthrough of feeling and willing is over and the
> almost undifferentiated affect-volition of early childhood
> has been replaced by the more highly developed feeling
> and willing, then thinking can free itself from its
> bondage. If at an earlier stage the child has paved the
> way towards objectivising the world, he now continues
> this objectivisation by confronting the world with the
> 'I' as something fully recognised, endowed with its own

feeling and willing. It can be called, 'person'. The author does not think she is wrong in regarding this time of crisis as the hour when the higher 'I' is born.[61]

However justified this whole description may be, the conclusion arrived at certainly seems unjustified. This time of crisis mentioned here is not the occasion of the 'I' or ego's birth, but the result of it. The ego is born in the awakening thinking, and the result of this event is the age of defiance that now follows. Neither is it the hour of the birth of the higher ego, but rather the death of it.[62] What now comes to light is the lower ego, which accompanies human beings through the whole of their earthly life.

Rudolf Steiner has characterised this moment in the light of spiritual science. He says:

> Clairvoyants, who can trace the spiritual processes involved because they have undergone spiritual training, discover that something tremendously significant happens at the moment when we achieve I-consciousness, that is, at the moment of our earliest memory. They can see that, during the early years of childhood, an aura hovers about us like a wonderful human-superhuman power. This aura, which is actually our higher part, extends everywhere into the spiritual world. But at the earliest moment we can remember, this aura penetrates more deeply into our inner being. We can experience ourselves as a coherent I from this point on because what had previously been connected to the higher worlds then entered the I. Thereafter, our consciousness establishes its own relationship to the outer world.[63]

This is an exact description of the spiritual process that lies hidden behind the events of the period of defiance.

The first great phase of childhood comes to an end, and will and impulse awaken at the birth of the lower ego.

We must gradually learn to see this phase of the first three years of childhood in a new light, not like Bühler and his successors, who consider children to be more or less animals that gradually grow out of the 'chimpanzee age' and have overtaken the 'whole phylogenetic animal evolution' by their third year.

Remplein, describing this phase, says:

> In the first phase those impulses and instincts of the
> body predominate that serve the mere preservation
> of life, but then they are joined by the impulses
> furthering the unfolding of the body-soul organism
> … This determination by instinct is the predominant
> characteristic of this whole stage.[64]

If that were the case, children would learn neither to walk nor to speak and think because these achievements in no way arise from the instinctual nature of infants. There is no other period in human life on earth as free from affect or instinct as that of the first three years. In this sense children are objective rather than wholly subjective beings. Even though they rest entirely within themselves, develop connections with the surrounding world only slowly, and gradually become individual personalities, children are hardly conscious of themselves and are therefore not selfish. They are each a world existing in themselves, and they may expect from the world around them everything that seems pleasant and acceptable to them. Where, however, do we find demands or even self-determination in small children? They accept what is given and by necessity relinquish what is withdrawn from them. Rudolf Steiner says:

In childhood, a dream world still seems to hover about us. We work on ourselves with a wisdom that is *not* in us, a wisdom that is more powerful and comprehensive than all the conscious wisdom we acquire later. This higher wisdom ... is obscured and exchanged for consciousness ... Something from this world [of the spirit] still flows into our aura during childhood. As individuals we are then directly subject to the guidance of the *entire* spiritual world to which we belong. When we are children – up to the moment of our earliest memory – the spiritual forces from this world flow into us, enabling us to develop our particular relationship to gravity. At the same time, the same forces also form our larynx and shape our brain into living organs for the expression of thought, feeling, and will.[65]

We meet here with those powers of wisdom that give children the faculties of walking, speaking, and thinking. In walking, children come to terms not only with the forces of gravity by overcoming them, but through this act they separate themselves as individual beings from the world of which they were formerly still a part. In speaking, children not only learn soul communication with other human beings, but take possession of things and beings in a new way so that they belong to them once more. Finally, in thinking, children once more acquire on a higher level what they have achieved in learning to walk. They lift themselves anew out of the world, but they are now more firm and consolidated. Like a shepherd they mingle again with the herd, which consists of the names of all things spread out around them. Children have regained them by giving them names, but now they themselves must not remain only a name. They enter the innermost being of the name by knowing how to name themselves beyond their given name. This is called 'I', and we thereby recognise

3. THE AWAKENING OF THINKING

ourselves as part of the World-I, which, as Logos, is the origin of all creation.[66]

It was for this reason that Rudolf Steiner said of this time of the first three years:

> Most meaningfully, therefore, the I-being of Christ[67] is expressed in the words: *'I am the Way, the Truth, and the Life!'* The higher spiritual forces form our organism in childhood – though we are not conscious of this – so that our body becomes the expression of the way, the truth and the life. Similarly, the human spirit gradually becomes the *conscious* bearer of the way, the truth and the life by permeating itself with Christ.[68]

4. The Unfolding of the Three Highest Senses

The senses of speech and thought

When we approach the question of how the human spirit unfolds in the course of early childhood with real courage, a special problem strikes us at once. We meet one of those great questions that appear repeatedly as hurdles for the thinker's courage to take in a single high jump.

This problem is the ever-new miracle that comes to pass at the beginning of children's second year: the spoken word is not only heard, but also grasped as a sign and its meaning understood. This understanding occurs long before children have developed the power of thinking! Thus, an intellectual activity is performed before the development of the faculties necessary for it. This is a miracle that impresses everyone except the psychologist who is lacking in philosophical training. Yet one of the most difficult questions of child psychology is how it is truly possible that words can be grasped, and their meaning understood, even in earliest childhood.[1] In his fundamental investigations of the development of speech in children, Stern has drawn our attention to a most important rule, which he formulated in the following way:

> From the innumerable words that the child continually
> hears, his mind makes an unconscious selection by
> discarding most and retaining only a few. This selection
> is twofold. The majority of rejected words are 'beyond
> understanding', and of these a smaller number have been
> rejected as 'beyond speech'. The retardation of what
> can be said with what can be understood is a peculiarity
> that continues even in adult years ... but nowhere is the
> difference as striking as in the first months of speech.[2]

Stern points to that threshold erected between hearing and understanding the spoken word. In the course of their first year children hear a great number of words and sentences, but do not yet comprehend them as independent parts, because they are still embedded in the 'experience landscapes' of which I have spoken in the second chapter of this book. Only at the end of the first and at the beginning of the second year does the word appear as symbol and as bearer of meaning in children's realm of consciousness.

These first words, or better, syllabic complexes, are not yet true words with sense and meaning, but are only expressions of what children want to indicate. The syllabic sequences are mostly still onomatopoeic designations like 'splash-splash' for bathing, 'bow-wow' for dog, 'yum-yum' for eating and so on. Children associate experienced values of feeling with them. When they say 'tick-tock', they may point to a clock, though without having grasped that they are saying the name of the object. As long as the period of one-word sentences and syllabic complexes lasts, that is, until about the middle of the second year, something spoken is only an expression or interpretation, such as pointing to an object or an event.

Nevertheless, we should pay close attention to what appears here because it is a kind of preparatory step towards true word understanding. The spoken word is distinguished from all other forms of sound production and is felt and noticed as speech. Tone and sound have become differentiated.[3] This is the first threshold, which leads to a further understanding of the spoken word. The crossing of the second threshold begins when children proceed from the period of 'saying' to that of 'naming'.

When, at about eighteen months, the joy of asking for the names of things, and then of pronouncing and using these names, awakens for children, the understanding of words begins and speech first assumes its rights. These fundamental differentiations have already been pointed out by Edmund Husserl[4] and later by Max Scheler.[5] Scheler's efforts have been especially helpful towards achieving clarity in this field:

> Between expression and speech the phenomenological findings show an absolute abyss ... Already the existence of a tone, sound or noise complex as 'sound' – though it be only 'one sound' outside in the passage, 'one sound' in the woods – requires that I perceive in this complex something more than its sense content that is 'expressed' in it, that is 'proclaimed aloud' in it. A 'sound', therefore, is already something quite different from tone, noise or a so-called association of such a complex with an imagined object. But the 'sound' still tarries in the sphere of pure expression ... a whole world separates even the most primitive word from mere expression. The entirely new thing that appears in the word is the fact that it does not, like the expression, merely point back to an experience, but in its primary function it points outwards to an object in the world. The word 'means' something that has nothing to do either with its sound-body, or with the experience of feelings, thoughts and ideas that it may express besides ... The word appears to us as the fulfilment of a demand made by the object itself.

> It appears in the understanding as a simple rather than a complex whole, which only the reflective analysis of the philologist or psychologist may later differentiate into the sound and the sense aspect (the 'word body' and 'word sense').[6]

I quote Scheler's statements at length because they go to the roots of a differentiation and separation to which Rudolf Steiner drew attention repeatedly and which in the future will become of fundamental importance for an understanding of human beings. It is significant that Scheler chooses his essay *On the Idea of Man* in which to come to grips with the problem of understanding and speaking.

Later, Ludwig Binswanger[7] tried to approach these problems from the standpoint of the neurologist and psychiatrist. He opens his essay *On the Problem of Speaking and Thinking* with the following statement:

> A homogenous phenomenon is the basis of the problem of speech and thought, from the simple, meaningful spoken or written word to speech proper, which in agreement with Husserl, we wish to call the sense-enlivened or sense-full expression. If we analyse this phenomenon, an undertaking that belongs to phenomenology, we can differentiate first the articulated complex of sounded or written physical signs; second, the psychic experiences in which man lends sense or meaning to these signs – the sense-giving and intentional actions; third, the ideal, logical sense or the meaning itself through which the expression points to an object or 'means' it.[8]

Though much in this formulation is incorrect and generalised, the reference to the three realms, physical, psychic and logical, clearly expresses the fact that speech must be understood only as a unity, as the synthesis of bodily, soul and spiritual relations. But as a result of this, to grasp and comprehend what is spoken must also be threefold. Whether I read what is written, or hear what is spoken, or whether I grasp signs and gestures, it is never an action of body and soul alone. If it were only that, no understanding through speech could ever come about.[9]

The miracle already mentioned, in which the first understanding of the heard word begins to dawn in small children, presupposes that the spiritual part of the childlike human being is precisely what is involved in the process of comprehending, and that even in earliest infancy a threshold of understanding is crossed that creates a real word from a sound formation.

Otherwise, how should it be possible that small children, seemingly without the slightest difficulty, begin to understand the word as sound gesture and directly grasp its hidden sense? A spiritual deed is the basis of such an event. Scheler and Husserl tried to point to this but in spite of the keenest observation of the phenomena in question they were not able to solve this riddle. Rudolf Steiner, however, reached a comprehensive answer to this problem by laying the foundation of a new theory of the senses.[10] As early as 1909 he described how the understanding of the spoken word should not be counted among the acts of cognition but among the sense activities. He showed how even to hear a spoken word is more than merely hearing and that a special sense underlies this faculty. He called this a speech or word sense, and the understanding of the spoken word he called the concept or thought sense. In the first descriptions of his theory of the senses he says:

> So we come to a ninth sense. We discover it when we
> think about the fact that there is indeed a certain capacity

of perception in the human being … a perceptive capacity that, although it is not based on judgment, is present in it. We perceive it when we use speech for the purpose of coming to an understanding with others. In what is conveyed to us through speech there is not simply an expression of judgment; a real speech sense underlies it … A child learns to speak before learning to reason.

And further on:

And now we come to the tenth sense, the highest among those used in ordinary life. It is our means for understanding concepts expressed through the medium of speech. It, too, is really a sense, just as the others are. We must have concepts to reason. If the soul is to become active it must be able to perceive concepts, which is possible through the sense of concept.[11]

Here a fundamentally new thought directs our previously existing views on the development of the human spirit along entirely unaccustomed paths. Not only a great number of existing problems can be solved with this,[12] but at the same time, new questions emerge that hitherto have hardly come into the light of our attention and awareness. In his book *Riddles of the Soul*, Steiner discussed in detail Franz Brentano's[13] psychology and then added a special chapter, *The True Basis of Intentional Relation*.[14] In it he develops important aspects of his theory of the senses. The following paragraph is particularly significant to our present considerations:

One believes, for example, that when hearing the words of another person, it suffices to speak of a 'sense' only insofar as 'hearing' comes into question and that everything else is to be ascribed to a non-sensory, inner activity. But that is not the actual state of affairs. In hearing human words and understanding them as thoughts, a threefold activity comes into consideration. And each component of this threefold activity must be studied in its own right if a valid scientific view is to arise. Hearing is one of these activities. But hearing as such is just as little a perception of words (*Vernehmen*) as touching is a seeing. And if, in accordance with the facts, one distinguishes between the sense of touch and the sense of sight, one must also make distinctions between hearing, perceiving words, and then apprehending thought. It leads to a faulty psychology and to a faulty epistemology if one does not make a sharp distinction between our apprehension of a thought and our thought activity, and if one does not recognise the sensory nature of the former. One makes this mistake only because the organ by which we perceive a word and that by which we apprehend a thought are not as outwardly perceptible as the ear is for hearing. In reality sense organs are present for these two activities of perception just as the ear is present for hearing.[15]

In this description Steiner brings into correct focus what we have described above in regard to Binswanger's exposition.[16] What is shown there as physical sign, as psychic experience and as logical sense, is basically a sense experience occurring in three differentiated sense realms. The physical sign is transmitted by the ear as the word that is heard, or by the eye as the word that is read. The psychic experience is the 'taking in of the word', and the logical sense the 'grasping of the thought'. How challenging are Rudolf Steiner's formulations to psychology and philosophy! They represent an entirely new phase in the history of the psychology and philosophy of speech and many critical investigations will have to be made to do justice to this tremendous impulse. Above all, the physiology of the senses will have to find a new orientation and entirely transform the views on the spiritual development of children.[17] The remaining sections of this chapter are meant to be a first attempt in this direction.

The development of the word sense and thought sense

There can hardly be any doubt that the word sense (comprehension of the spoken word) and the thought sense (comprehension of concepts) both develop in children during the first two years if their development takes a fairly normal course. At the end of their first year children already begin to use one-word sentences with understanding and comprehend some of the words addressed to them. At the end of their second year, when they begin to say two- or three-word sentences, they already know a large number of words, recognise their sense and meaning and can use them accordingly. The word as formation and sign has become their permanent possession. Children have made the first roots of language their own, but only because the senses of speech and thought have awakened in them.

To gain some understanding of these two senses it will be necessary to study their development in connection with that of the speech of children. The unfolding of language in children must be intimately connected with the acquisition of these two senses because it is obvious that newborn children possess neither word nor thought sense. Both certainly are present as predispositions, but the development of speech is needed to turn them into faculties.

In the second chapter of this book, we pointed out that the first year is of the greatest importance for the formation of speech. We said that the development of speech begins with the first cry and after that infants soon start to utter a great variety of sounds. They cry and crow, gurgle and coo, and at the end of the first month most parents have learned to 'understand' the various sounds and noises. For example, Charles Valentine,[18] an accurate observer, writes:

> At the end of the first month I could distinguish three types of sounds. First, the cry of hunger, which was restless and sharp, increased each time and after the last strong outbreak suddenly ceased. Second, the cry of pain, which was a much stronger and more lasting cry. Third, a satisfied contented gurgling, which was different in its sound formation in the three children observed.[19]

The cry in this instance is nothing but statement. It is an expression of well-being or misery and as yet has hardly any connection to speech as such. This relationship, however, is already being established in the second or third month. About this Valentine writes:

> When father or mother chatted to the baby, humming was returned in reply. That happened with Y. on the twenty-second, with B. on the thirty-second and with A. on the forty-ninth day for the first time. Thus speech development was even at this time connected with social relationships.[20]

Valentine mentions that some observers put the beginning of this 'responding' on the part of babies later, especially when the children being observed did not come under observation in their family milieu. But most found that it began around the middle or end of the second month.

Here we witness how babies react with understanding upon being addressed for the first time. They answer the speech of another person with their own utterances, demonstrating their use of their own speech organs through imitation. In this we can see a first understanding for the act of speaking.

In the course of the third month the sounds and tones that children utter become quite diversified and consist of recognisable consonants as well as vowels. Again, Valentine says:

> By this stage of three months it became quite evident from the number of sounds made by these children, which we could never have pronounced, that the speech of the child was largely independent of the words he heard.[21]

This is a further and most important conclusion because it shows that the hearing at this infantile age does not yet work together with the activities of the larynx and other speech organs. A child hears with their ears and, independently of this, makes utterances with their larynx and their other developing speech organs. The 'intentional relations' between these two activities have not yet developed and only another person can make a baby's speech organs respond when they address the baby directly.

From about the fourth month on, however, infants begin to imitate sounds and noises they have heard and, once they have achieved this, make them their own by continued exercise. Now the time begins when during waking hours children babble continually and keep repeating certain sounds and sound complexes. Around the sixth month, this 'conscious' imitation of sounds they have heard becomes a daily event. Infants have now reached the stage when ears and speech organs can work as a functional whole. This is an important step, and a prattling comprehension of the sounds of their native language begins.[22]

Valentine describes a most striking phenomenon that he observed in his own children and that thousands of other parents may also have observed without noticing. He points out that the sounds imitated at will are always spoken only in a whisper. He says, 'These deliberate imitations, however, were strikingly different from the spontaneous and the deferred imitative speaking. They were whispered.'[23] This behaviour occurs at about the eighth month.

William Preyer[24] also describes whispering by his child in whom it occurred in the tenth or eleventh month:

> When I spoke, the child, observing my lips attentively, often made the attempt to speak after me. Usually some different sound came forth, however, or there was merely a soundless movement of the lips.[25]

This description makes it clear why only whispering or silent lip movements occur. A child looks at the movements of an adult's mouth and imitates the movement but not the sounds. They can indeed prattle aloud unconsciously and unconsciously imitate the sounded tones of speech. Conscious repetition, however, occurs at first only in the interaction of their observation of mouth movements, that is, the interaction between their eyes and their motor impulses.

Towards the end of the first year a significant new step is taken in development. In describing it, Preyer points out that children not only react to tones, noises and sounds at this time, but they may also turn in the direction of a speaker when their name is called. At every new sound that they have not yet heard they are astonished and show this by opening their eyes and mouth wide.

By frequently repeating the words, 'Shake hands,' and simultaneously holding out his hand, Preyer even induced his child to comply with this request. The beginning of word memory was thereby established.

Most other observers agree with these conclusions that towards the end of the first year a few words are understood and the movements corresponding to them are executed. Thus, Valentine's child 'Y' was able to look at the floor when hearing the word 'kitty' in order to search for the cat, and at the word 'birdie' to look at the wall where birds were depicted on the wallpaper. They also understood the words 'bottle', 'mouth', 'bye-bye' and a few others, and performed characteristic gestures relative to them.

Stern relates the following of his child, Eva, when twelve and thirteen months old:

> We are continually astounded and can scarcely keep up with her development. It is hardly credible at her age. One day she will grasp the meaning of a word a little, the next, a little more, the following day she will understand it entirely. All at once we noticed that the child understood perfectly what we said.[26]

Similarly, Preyer remarks:

> The most important progress consists in the awakened understanding of spoken words. The ability to learn has emerged almost overnight. Suddenly, it did not require constant repetition of the question, 'How tall is the child?' at the same time lifting her arms in order to get her to make the movement each time she heard, 'How tall' or 'all' or even, 'a'.[27]

When we try to interpret these details of child speech development during the first year with regard to the word sense as well as the thought sense, we can note a steady development. At first, the sound utterances of children are entirely spontaneous and only an expression of the experience of their own existence. In the second month, children respond by humming when spoken to. They become dimly aware of the movements of their own mouths. This is a sense perception that belongs in the realm of motor sensations and is concentrated in the region of the mouth.

In the third month the variety of sounds and tones that children can produce spontaneously is extended, and from the fourth month on they begin to imitate definite sounds that they have heard. This ability is more firmly established in the course of the following months, with no new fundamental acquisition being added until the seventh or eighth months. Around this time children begin to imitate at will the words and sounds spoken to them. This imitation primarily involves the interaction of eyes and lips and is related to the lip reading of the deaf and hard of hearing, which has its origin here. This process, therefore, takes place softly or quite voicelessly. A combination of the sense of sight with motor sensation, which produces movement of the mouth, is also present, bringing about a further development of consciousness in the region of the lips and mouth.[28] Thus, another step is taken in the development of the ability to respond.

Towards the end of the first year, beginning at about the ninth month, a kind of intuitive comprehension of the word as designation arises. Many authors speak of this as a 'word understanding', but that is by no means the case. As shown above, all these 'understood' words are clothed in gestures that imitate repeated sound structures. These sound structures are certainly remembered but not yet understood. Memory alone enables children to experience sound structures as speech symbols and to connect them with the respective gestures, sensations and objects. When little Eva Stern at thirteen months used the word 'doll' for her doll and all pictures of children, it was a recognition of definitely established connections. These were by no means identifications for her that revealed a 'name' through word or sound structure. It was rather a case in which she was able to remember and recognise definite, self-chosen sound formations and words. One should not fall into the error of considering this accomplishment to be a form of the cognitive process. It is a simple recognition and not an understanding of the word and its meaning. Nevertheless, it is a new achievement of great importance to the further development of speech.

Anyone familiar with the teaching and education of deaf children knows that one of the greatest and often insurmountable difficulties is to awaken in the deaf and those unable to speak their sleeping word memory. They learn relatively soon to hear and differentiate tones and sounds but the difficulties experienced in 'marking', 'be-thinking', and 'recollecting' words represent one of the greatest obstacles to the acquisition of somewhat normal, colloquial speech. Children who can hear achieve these abilities 'suddenly' and 'overnight'. But this happens only at that time when they have acquired their upright position. Word and sound memory awaken only after the development of uprightness.

While the word is consciously separated for the first time, it is sorted out in a twofold way. On the one hand, the word is lifted out of the realm of other sounds and noises and remembered independently. On the other hand, however, it is drawn away from the motor sphere and treated as an independent world.[29] All these observations demonstrate that in the course of their first year children gradually learn to experience word and sound formations, and then come to know them at the beginning of the second year as self-contained entities. Around the time that children raise themselves up, the word also emerges from the motor organism and from the other sounds with which it was formerly intermingled. The liberations of two activities have occurred simultaneously. Children have learned to stand upright on the earth, and, when they begin to speak, the word rises up like a lark into the free and breathing air.

When, together with the acquisition of the upright position, the word also gains its independence, the word sense is born. With its separation from the other motor and sensory regions, the word, although not yet recognised in its independent form as thought, is received like a sense perception. The faculty of word memory is indeed already the result of the developed word sense. Here, at the beginning of the second year, stands the cradle of the word sense. Rudolf Steiner expresses it in the following way:

> Because the sensation of phonetic tone precedes using
> mental judgment, children learn to sense the meaning of
> the tone of words before they can use judgment. In fact,
> they learn judgment by way of language.[31]

Now, from direct experience communicated to them by the speech sense, children know that a word is different from any other sound that reaches them through their hearing. The word is born as an independent entity and is laid into the cradle of the word sense.

Children spend the next six months practising the use of the newly acquired sense of word or speech. They do not learn many additional new words and sound structures, but rather make their own what they have suddenly been able to achieve. Therefore, remarkably, few new words are acquired during this period.

At this time, too, the acquisition and development of a special faculty occurs. This is important because it points to the awakened sense of speech. Valentine writes:

> I have already mentioned that in B. and Y. only two examples of true gesture language appeared before the end of the first year. It is well-known that the deaf develop an extensive language of gestures to compensate for the absence of a language of sound. An experienced teacher of deaf children told me that lip reading and attempts to speak are delayed in deaf children if gestures are allowed to continue.[32] There are also records of children who continued gesture language because of slowness in acquiring speech ... Among the Dionne quintuplets gestures were remarkably expressive and fairly common, and these children had difficulty with speech.[33]

Valentine then gives many examples of how, after the completion of the first year, sound and gesture language can vicariously replace each other.

The following words of Rudolf Steiner should be considered in this context:

> We must also take into account that audible tone is not alone in revealing to us an inwardness such as that present in tone of speech. In the end, gestures, mimicry, and facial expressions also lead us to something simple and direct that must be included,[34] along with the content of any audible tone, in the domain of the sense of word.[35]

This is a confirmation of the fact that true gestures begin to appear as gesture language only after the birth of the sense of speech.[36]

All onomatopoeic sounds that children begin to use are not really words but sound gestures, repeated in imitation of sounds they have heard, especially in imitation of words spoken to them. The memory of sound becomes more fixed and is combined with perceptions from other sensory realms, especially that of the eyes. Picture books can now be read because children take the greatest delight in connecting their illustrations with the words belonging to them. The word, it is true, is not yet 'understood', but it is remembered; it has become perception and idea. Because the word sense has developed as sense activity, it has begun to perceive the word and to transform this perception into an idea.

When in the second half of the second year children enter the first age of questioning and make such startling progress in the second stage of speech development, when they begin to ask the names of things and beings and acquire the new words as quickly as possible by simple repetition, it seems as if true thought action might be appearing in them. Thus, Stern writes:

> The occurrence just described must undoubtedly be considered as a mental act of the child in the real sense of the word. The insight into the relation between sign and import that the child gains here is something fundamentally different from simply dealing with perceptions and their associations. The demand that some name must belong to every object, whatever its nature, may be considered as a real – perhaps the child's first – general thought.[37]

Stern, however, though he comes from the school of Brentano and Husserl, falls victim to one of those fatal confusions that lead to incomprehension of the independently active thought sense. It is impossible to expect from two-year-old children a 'general' act of thinking, and to imagine that they logically comprehend that everything has a name. Although children later become aware of this fact, it is due not to an act of cognition but to one of perception when the word sense is joined by the thought sense. Rudolf Steiner says:

> Indeed, there also exists a *direct and immediate perception* for that which is revealed in a concept, so that we must speak of a *sense of concept*. What we can experience within our own soul as a concept, we can also receive as revealed from an external being.[38]

It is this that begins to be unveiled in two-year-old children. Words become gates and windows for looking into the world of ideas, and children can perceive these ideas even if they cannot yet think them.

Stern also points out that with 'naming', the third root of speech tendency – the 'intentional' one as he calls it – begins to work. But these intentional relations are acts that occur between the different sense regions. They are not soul processes belonging to the region of thought. When seen from another side, it becomes even clearer that we are concerned here with an awakening – one could almost say, the first dawning of the thought sense. In the second part of these investigations, we dealt briefly with the so-called 'change of meaning' of words in this phase of development. We drew attention to the fact that these are by no means chance designations but that children draw the contours of a comprehensive concept as an idea much more ingeniously than grown-ups are able to do. Valentine[39] gives some relevant examples of fundamental importance, to each of which I have added the necessary comments:

> E.W. uses at fifteen months (!) the word 'door' for doors, garden gates and water taps.

Here we have a grasp of things that can be 'opened'. This is a much wider concept than the single words would indicate by themselves. The idea of 'opening' is represented by the word 'door'.

> B. at nineteen months first calls a sparrow 'dickie' and then all birds, later still all flies, spiders and bits of fluff floating in the air.

Again, we have a comprehensive idea, 'flying', and the name 'dickie' is given to everything that flies or has the potentiality of flying.

> B. at twenty months first says 'go(ne)' when objects disappear, or food is finished. He says it again when he has had enough food and pushes the rest away.

The passive use of 'go' becomes an active one produced at will. The meaning has not changed at all; it was well-defined from the beginning, but always broad and general.

> Another child at seventeen months uses the word 'eijebapp' (for *eisenbahn*, meaning railway), which until then was a designation only for his toy railway and for some dogs lined up in a row.[40]

Here we can easily discover the identity of form impressions and their naming with the same word. But we cannot call this deeds of thinking, but rather identifications that show the 'idea' of a word to have been grasped, but grasped as form, as perception. On the other hand, there are also many instances where the comprehension of the idea of a word has been too narrow, when children, for instance, apply the word 'armchair' only to one definite type of chair, but do not recognise those of unfamiliar form.

Many more examples could be given but the principle presented here shows that at about eighteen months children begin to develop their thought sense in addition to the already perfected sense of speech. This sense activity starts rather suddenly because the thought sense is awakened at the moment when the names of things have become experiences. It might also be said that at the moment the thought sense awakens in children all things receive a name. In this way, by becoming bearers of names, words assume their meaning. The further development of the thought sense occurs in a slightly different form from that of the sense of speech, which grows firmer and stronger because no new words were acquired. In the case of the thought sense, however, a rapid acquisition of new words occurs, making it possible to grasp as comprehensively as possible the images of ideas in all their manifoldness.

These images of ideas can be conceived by children either more broadly or more narrowly than in their later correspondence to fully developed speech. They are, however, in no way arbitrary. They only differ in dimension, which is directly related to the breadth of each child's soul existence, which expands beyond their true being, and with the narrowness of their earthly bodily existence in which they are a child. This continues its expression right into the awakening and handling of the thought sense.

One of the most moving examples of the awakening of the thought sense can be seen in the way the seven-year-old Helen Keller[41] suddenly grasped an understanding of words. Her teacher, Anne Sullivan,[42] reports:

> We went out to the pumphouse, and I made Helen hold her mug under the spout while I pumped. As the cold water gushed forth, filling the mug, I spelled 'w-a-t-e-r' into Helen's free hand. The word coming so close upon the sensation of cold water rushing over her hand seemed

to startle her. She dropped the mug and stood as one transfixed. A new light came over her face. She spelled 'w-a-t-e-r' several times. Then she dropped to the ground, asking for the name of the earth and that of the pump and trellis. Suddenly turning around, she asked for my name. I spelled, 'teacher'. At this moment the nurse came to the pumphouse with Helen's little sister. Helen spelled 'baby' and pointed to the nurse. This was the first time she used a word spelled out as means of communication by herself. On the way back to the house she was in great excitement and learned the name of every object she touched so that she had added some thirty new words to her vocabulary within a few hours. Some of them were 'door', 'open', 'shut', 'give', 'go', and 'come'.[43]

The next morning Anne Sullivan added a postscript to the letter she had written the previous evening. It read:

Helen got up this morning like a radiant fairy. She flew from one object to another, asked for the names of everything and, full of joy, kissed me. Last night when she went to bed, quite on her own she snuggled into my arms and kissed me for the first time. I thought my heart would break, so full of joy was it.

Here we must bear in mind that for weeks previous the teacher of this deaf and blind child had inscribed the names of things into Helen Keller's hand in sign language. She could repeat them, but she could not grasp or perceive them. They were signs without meaning. Her speech sense existed as gesture sense. Suddenly, however, as if by revelation, her thought sense awakened and from that moment on – that world moment – her spirit being was at home on the earth.[44] She could, like Adam, call things by their names. A new light transfigured her face because the light of the spirit had awakened in her and radiated from her.

A similar joy, which is not so immediate because it does not awake so suddenly, also illuminates a two-year-old child. They are accepted here on earth as a human being through the fact that they can comprehend the names of things. They have become an Adam.

The physical organ of the sense of speech

Now that we have described the unfolding of the senses of speech and of thought in the light of speech development, we can take a further step towards an understanding of these phenomena.

It is indeed new and somewhat startling to have to accept the fact that everything hitherto regarded as a complicated act of thinking is reduced to a simple sense experience. Thus, a small child does not think the meaning of the words they acquire but perceives it through their senses. This may be difficult to accept because the words 'sentient' or 'sense experience' are so narrowly bound up with our habitual way of thinking about them. For us, 'sense' or 'sentient' is everything connected with those experiences that we have in the outer world where we see, hear, smell, and taste the qualities of the things we perceive.

We also have sensations of pain, hunger and thirst, and we dimly experience our equilibrium in space and the position of our limbs relative to each other.[45] These are sense experiences that we continually receive. With them our sensation of life and existence is most intimately connected. These sense perceptions, however, are experiences that, although vague and dull and not entering directly into the field of consciousness, are nevertheless significant. For the loss of equilibrium or a disturbance in feeling the position of our limbs or a diminished sensation of pain, can lead to the most serious impairment of our existence. They are at least symptoms of deep-seated illness. These sense experiences of our body and soul conditions, to which we must add our feelings of well-being or discomfort, belong to the sphere of sense processes.

Even for the latter we can still accept the word 'sentient' in its general characterisation. Our body is only part of the 'outer world', and we can experience it as such by means of a special group of senses. We not only see it partly from outside and hear it speak and sing, but we feel its condition quite directly in pleasure and pain, in being well or unwell, and we know this to be so not only for ourselves but for everyone.

How is something supposed to become the content of our senses that lies beyond the 'sense' world and reveals itself only as thought? It is still possible to retain some of the 'sense' character of the perception in the word sense since this represents only a kind of widened sense of hearing. What is revealed in hearing as a single sound or tone becomes, in the homogeneous perception of a sound, complex in the word sense.

In the sound of a vowel or consonant many single sounds are joined that the word sense (or sense of speech) comprehends as a whole, as a homogeneous form. Just as through the sense of hearing we can grasp a melody from single tones, so through the medium of the sense of speech we can perceive a word or succession of words from the joining of single sounds.

After this has happened, another sphere is opened and through the word we are supposed to sense and perceive the meaning it expresses. Everything that precedes this process in the field of perception is of a different character, since a thing or a being tastes, smells, has colour and form, utters tones and sounds – all of which are qualities of its existence. Even the name it bears still belongs to it and is part of its character and existence. The idea, the concept that is it, itself, however, is not a part or a portion, but much more than that. It is something indivisible, the *ens*[46] itself. It can well bear different names, it can be called, 'dog', but it can also be called, *canis, chien* or *Hund*. It can have many such names, just as it can have an infinite number of attributes. But 'the' dog, the dog-hood, is contained in each name, in each attribute, so that it is a uniform whole in all its differentiation. Is this indivisibleness (which, when it is ourselves, we call 'I') supposed to be given to us as perception, so that not only qualities but even the bearer of these qualities is supposed to become our immediate experience?

Yet how would an understanding be possible between human beings if this immediate experience did not exist? Can it be imagined that thinking can be measured in any other way except by the perception of concepts and ideas? The prevailing view that from our manifold experiences we gain the necessary concepts through gradual abstraction cannot be upheld. We can only begin to comprehend the miracle of word understanding in children, if in our consistent investigation of the spheres of the senses we also include those that bring to our experience not only the qualities of the things but their *ens* itself.

When this is understood, a further, weighty problem confronts us that results from the question: if for every sense process hitherto known, an organ can be found in the body, where do the senses of speech and thought have their physical organisation? Nothing is known about this even though there is no part of our body that has not been thoroughly investigated anatomically down to the last detail.[47] Since it is a case of sense processes, however, we must ask about the sense organs pertaining to them.

Only after these have been found, examined, and investigated, can the senses of speech and thought reveal themselves as 'comprehensible' entities.

In his *Riddles of the Soul*, Rudolf Steiner outlined the nature of the senses of speech and thought and added the following remarks:

> It leads to a faulty psychology and to a faulty epistemology if one does not make a sharp distinction between our apprehension of a thought and our thought activity, and if one does not recognise the sensory nature of the former. One makes this mistake only because the organ by which we perceive a word and that by which we apprehend a thought are not as outwardly perceptible as the ear is for hearing. In reality sense organs are present for these two activities of perception just as the ear is present for hearing.[48]

The spiritual investigator, as we see, has no doubts about the existence of physical organs either for word sense or thought sense, and these two functions can become really effective only through them. Is it at all possible to find these organs in the multitude of the morphological structures of the human body? So far no one in science has even thought of these two senses, let alone tried to assign working organs to them. It could be, however, that the functions of certain well-known morphological structures have been misinterpreted and activities attributed to them that they do not really perform. In other words, special parts of our body could be the organs of our senses of thought and speech that have not yet been recognised as such because these senses themselves are still unknown.

If this surmise is true, it will not be a question of finding a 'new' organ because the human body has been completely investigated macroscopically as well as microscopically.

What will be necessary is a new interpretation of the existing organ and tissue structures so that they appear in a new order and shape. Then a number of organs to which no common basic design has hitherto been attributed may be recognised that will form the physical organisation we hope to find.[49] Here we have reached an important point of departure to which we want to hold fast for the time being.

Looking back on our past considerations, we found that the unfolding of the sense of speech occurs exactly at the end of the first year, and the thought sense breaks through in the course of the second year. In these periods of development, children acquire an upright position, the ability to walk and the faculty of speech. Does the sense of speech appear at the end of the first year because it is intimately bound up with the acquisition of the ability to walk? Indeed, is it not conceivable that the human being's ability to walk upright is the prerequisite for the sense of speech? Could this perhaps be the reason why so many children who have difficulties in acquiring an upright position also find it hard to acquire speech and speech understanding? Is this the reason why an intimate connection exits between human motor activities and the sense of speech? Can only the acquisition of the ability to walk upright build the organ that then acts as the sense organ for the understanding of words?

A serious consideration of such questions can lead to the further deliberation that the acquisition of walking, as described in the first chapter of this book, is the product of the human being gradually gaining control of their voluntary muscles by means of their own self. In the course of the first year, this process builds up a distinct organ as part of our nervous system that is called the 'pyramidal system'. It consists of groups of nerves that extend from the voluntary muscles of the limbs and the trunk into the spinal cord, where they come into contact with another group of nerves running up the spinal cord and terminate in definite locations in the cortical regions of the cerebrum. This whole complex of nerves, extending from the cortex via the spinal cord to the single muscles, is described as the pyramidal system. It is a highly complex and extensive organ, which constitutes an essential part of our nervous system.

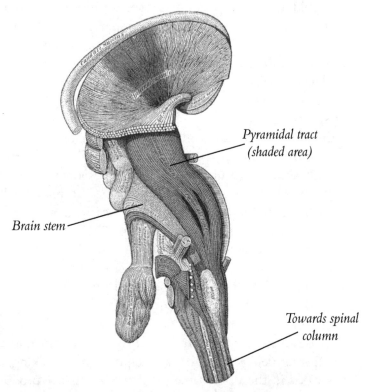

The pyramidal tract. The complex of nerves extends from the cortex down through the brain stem (where they cross the midline) and into the spinal cord. From there nerves branch out to the individual muscles in the body to form the pyramidal system.

Until quite recently, physiologists and neurologists were firmly convinced that this was a group of motor nerves that caused voluntary muscular movements. Of late, however, strong objections have been raised against this conception both in physiology and neurology. Clinical observations of the ill and the results of extensive brain operations have shown that these motor nerves function as such only under certain conditions. Movements that are experimentally induced through these nerves differ decidedly in form and character from normal movements, which are suppressed by artificial stimulation of the pyramidal system.[50] Modern neurology is thus faced with a riddle, which at present it hardly dares to admit, let alone to try to solve. This most 'human' of all nerve groupings, collectively called the 'pyramid tract', is functionally unrecognised today. We know its pathological performance when it fails through injury or illness, but its normal function is veiled in darkness.[51]

Thus, we see in the pyramidal system a morphological entity, a group of nerves that apparently does not perform the function hitherto assigned to it. Though closely connected with voluntary movements, it certainly is not the cause of them. This morphological entity is formed during the first year of life, but once its formation is completed it seems to be no longer directly connected with the functional achievement of walking upright and the voluntary mobility associated with it. The nerve apparatus thus formed has taken an intimate part in the acquisition of the ability to walk upright, but when this is achieved, it begins to place itself at the disposal of new functions. This is a form of functional change that should be noted.[52]

Rudolf Steiner gives a description in which he explains the nature and form of the physical organ of the sense of speech:

Furthermore, we are able to initiate movement from within ourselves. We have the power to express all the movements of our inner nature through movement – through hand movements, for example, or by the way we turn our head or move it up or down. Now, the basis for our ability to bring our bodies into movement is provided by the physical organism. This is not the physical organism of life, but the physical organism that provides us with the ability to move.[53]

Steiner means something quite specific here. He is not referring to movement that appears as voluntary motor activity, but to the physical organisation through which mobility manifests itself. Is he not referring to the pyramidal system? This system, as we have seen, is not the cause of voluntary movements, yet they are executed in connection with it. Then Steiner adds:

This [organism of the faculty of movement] is also the organ for perceiving speech, for perceiving the words which others address to us. We would not be able to understand a single word if we did not possess the physical apparatus of movement. It is really true: in sending out nerves for apprehending the whole process of movement, our central nervous system also provides us with the sensory apparatus for perceiving the words that are spoken to us.[54]

These words only confirm what I have tried to describe above because the nerves that are sent out for 'apprehending the whole process of movement' are without doubt the nerves of the pyramidal system. We have, therefore, to seek the sense organ of the sense of speech in the pyramidal path and in the nerve structures belonging to it. Here is a thousandfold instrument whose strings are strung between the muscles and the brain and in their totality serve our understanding of speech.

This view has been confirmed by clinical research carried out by the director of the Neurological Clinic in Hamburg. Klaus Conrad[55] made extensive investigations into the localisation of certain speech disturbances in the brain.[56] He was able to show that these aphasic disturbances occur at the time when the cerebrum has been injured or destroyed in those parts known to be the regions in which the pyramidal system has its origin, and that these aphasic disturbances are mostly those that have to do with a partial or complete loss of speech understanding. Such patients are either unable to understand words addressed to them or they lose the faculty of speaking. The latter state is conditioned by the fact that the comprehension of word forms has been preserved only in part or not at all.

We have now gained a fundamental insight into the phenomenology of the sense of speech. We have recognised its intimate connection with the acquisition of the ability to walk upright and have described its physical organ, which is a purely nervous one consisting only of nerve tissue. The entire system of voluntary muscles is found at the ends of the nerves, and though it is held together by the pyramidal system, it is neither functionally activated nor moved by it.[57] The pyramidal tract has become the organ of the word sense through the fact that it belongs to the voluntary motor apparatus as a whole, yet does not move it. On the contrary, it rests quietly within itself. This is the change of function that has occurred here.

Rudolf Steiner describes this:

> Suppose I make a movement like this [a hand raised
> in a gesture of holding off]. Now, even the smallest
> of movements is not just localised in one part of
> the organism, but comes from the entire movement

organism. And when you consider this motion as
coming from the entire movement organism, it has a
very particular effect. When another person expresses
something in words, I am doing what I need to do to
understand it by not making this gesture. Because I do
not make this gesture, but repress it instead, I am able to
understand what someone else is saying; my movement
organism wakes up right to the tips of my fingers, but I
hold back the motion, delay it, block it. By blocking this
motion, I am enabled to understand what is being said.[58]

Here we are given a foundation for an understanding of
the function of the word sense. We are shown that it is the
movement that is not executed, the gesture that does not
express itself, that conveys the understanding of the word
addressed to us. The non-accomplished intention, which
eliminates itself *in statu nascendi* and keeps still instead of
moving, is the basis of our word sense. [59]

This occurrence can be compared with resonance.
When I sing a certain sequence of tones into a piano, they
echo back softly. This does not happen when the strings
are in vibration, but only when they are at rest. In the same
way the spoken word resounds in me when I suppress
the movement of its gesture instead of executing it. This
happens only through that organ called the pyramidal
system, that complex bundle of countless nerves that acts
like a damper or mute. It does not execute the voluntary
movement but holds it back, thus becoming the instrument
in which the spoken word finds its echo or resonance.
Understanding the word is the result.[60]

Now we also see why the threshold of children's
understanding of speech is higher than that of speaking.
This was indicated when the development of speech
was described. At the end of the first year children have
learned, with the help of the pyramidal system they have

developed, to suppress certain gesture movements, and have thus advanced to the understanding of words. They have still not learned speech itself, however, because the understanding of words, the acquisition of the word sense, is a necessary prerequisite for the formation of the motor activity of speaking, that is, the speech movement itself. As long as children babble, they have not developed a word sense. The gradual transformation of babbling into speaking occurs only after this development. This must be clearly seen, otherwise, we cannot fully understand the growth of children's minds. The sense of speech is born through the acquisition of the ability to walk upright, and only through the birth of the sense of speech can speaking unfold.

Rudolf Steiner has often indicated that speaking is formed from the entire voluntary motor activity. In his lecture from which we have been quoting, he describes it in the following way:

> If we use spiritual-scientific means to investigate the
> human being, we discover that the things on which the
> capacity to speak and the capacity for understanding speech
> are based are very closely related to one other … Speaking
> originates in the realm of the soul; the will kindles speech
> in the soul. Naturally, no words would ever be spoken
> if our will were not active, if we did not develop will
> impulses. Observing a person spiritually-scientifically,
> we can see that what happens in them when he speaks is
> similar to what happens when they understand something
> that is being spoken. But what happens when a person
> themselves speaks involves a much smaller portion of
> the organism, much less of the organism of movement.
> Remember that the entire organism of movement must
> be taken into account in the case of the sense of speech,
> the sense of word … A part of it, a part of the movement
> organism, is isolated and brought into motion when we

speak. The larynx is the principal organ of this isolated portion of the organism of movement, and speaking occurs when will impulses rouse the larynx into motion. When we ourselves speak, what happens in our larynx happens because impulses of will originating in our soul bring the part of our movement organism that is concentrated in the larynx into motion. The entire movement organism, however, is the sense organ for understanding speech; but we keep it still while we are perceiving words.[61]

Steiner here points to the fact that the 'movement organism', the resting part of which (the pyramidal system) we have recognised as the organ of the sense of speech, bears speech most intimately within it. The speech process, however, is concentrated in the speech organs, which arrange themselves around the larynx, and the muscles of tongue, cheeks, jaw, and larynx are activated within the motor organism.

The physical organ of the sense of thought

Our considerations have reached the point at which we can say that in the course of speech development, the thought sense unfolds. It happens during a child's second year and the relation of the formation of the thought sense to the acquisition of speech is similar to the relation of the formation of the word sense to the acquisition of the ability to walk upright. In our search for the organ of the thought sense, can we conclude that the connection of this organ to the speech organs is similar to the intimate connection of the organ of the speech sense with motor ability? To arrive at an answer, we must examine the nerve supply of the larynx and its complicated muscular apparatus.

The muscles of the larynx present a kind of muscular system in miniature, and in their manifoldness and complexity of arrangement they make possible all the finer movements necessary for the act of speaking. The muscles of the abdomen, chest, back and limbs are reduced in number and size in the larynx, and they are also simplified and drawn together as if in a knot. Yet they render possible the endless variety of muscular combinations needed for the production of the singing and speaking voice in all its modulation. This motor system in miniature is supplied by two major nerve branches that come from above and below. They penetrate the larynx in pairs on both its right and left sides where they branch out to connect with the muscles and other tissues.

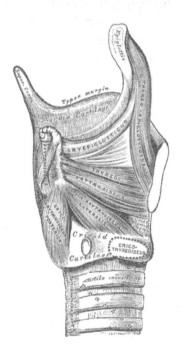

The muscles of the larynx.

Physiologists have lost their sense of wonder for the fact that these two nerve branches are stems of the vagus nerve, which is one of the twelve cranial nerves. The vagus nerve is special among the cranial nerves because it alone belongs to the autonomic nervous system. This is the plexus that is spread out over the body and regulates the large organs, the blood vessels and the circulation of fluids through the tissues. Its function mainly controls those processes occurring in the subconscious. The excretions of the large glands, the heartbeat, the muscular movements of stomach and intestines, the tension of blood vessels are all governed by the autonomic nervous system. What goes on in this dim realm is regulated by the vagus nerve and is brought to our waking consciousness only when conditions of illness become known through pain, discomfort, and sensations like hunger and thirst. It is from this nerve, which belongs to the vegetative layers of our existence, that branches pass to the larynx and regulate speech, one of the highest of human achievements.

This most extraordinary phenomenon demands our full attention. Speaking is an entirely voluntary, motor act and yet, in contrast to all other voluntary movements, it is not bound to the nerves of the pyramidal system. On the contrary, important as it is to human existence, through its nerve supply it belongs to the dull vegetative strata. This can be explained by the fact that the larynx is not part of the muscular apparatus but belongs to the respiratory system. To say this, however, only bridges the abyss produced by the problems of this form complex. The abyss itself remains unexplored. Yet, an understanding of this strange phenomenon should be sought.[62]

In a beautiful essay, Rudolf Treichler[63] has shown that the totality of the autonomic nervous system is intimately connected with the sense of life, and that one is even justified in speaking of this nervous system as the organ of

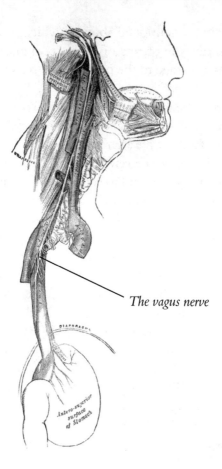

The vagus nerve

The vagus nerve serves the regulation of the autonomic
nervous system, which governs unconscious, internal
processes such as heart rate and digestion.

perception for the sense of life.[64] We can, therefore, ascribe
to the totality of our manifestations and processes of life the
realm of the vegetative or autonomic system, from which
certain sensations, such as hunger and thirst, comfort and
discomfort and other bodily sensations reach the threshold
of consciousness.

127

In the lecture mentioned above in which Rudolf Steiner tries to describe the organs of the three highest senses, he also devotes a passage to the organ of the sense of thought:

> Now we come to the sense of thought. What is the organ
> for perceiving the thoughts of others? Everything that we
> are, in so far as we are aware of the stirrings of life within
> us, is our organ for perceiving others' thoughts. Think of
> yourself, not with regard to your form, but with regard
> to the life you bear within you. Your whole organism is
> permeated with life. This life is a unity. In so far as the
> life of our entire organism is expressed physically, it is
> the organ for perceiving thoughts that come towards us
> from without ... we would not be able to perceive the
> thoughts of another if we did not bear life in the way
> that we do. Here I am not talking about the sense of
> life. What is in question here is not the inner perception
> of our general vital state of being – and that is what the
> sense of life gives us – rather is it the extent to which we
> are bearers of life. And it is the life we bear within us,
> the physical organism that bears the life within us, that is
> the organ by which we perceive the thoughts that others
> share with us.[65]

These indications of Rudolf Steiner clearly show that he saw the organ of the sense of thought in the region of 'activity' and 'life' in us, in those regions that belong to the autonomic nervous system. Can we imagine that this weaving of constructive and destructive life processes is itself the organ of the sense of thought? Steiner makes a definite reservation here when he says, and even repeats, that he means life 'in so far as the life of our entire organism is expressed physically' or 'the physical organism that bears the life within us'. How should this be understood?

Thorough research has gradually led physiologists and neurologists to distinguish two different parts of the autonomic nervous system – a sympathetic and a parasympathetic region. Quite different functions, which are polar opposites, are attributed to them. The sympathetic system exerts a stimulating effect and the parasympathetic system a calming one. A host of theories and assumptions have been built upon these polar functions of the autonomic nervous system. Rudolf Max Hess,[66] who has spent his life with these questions, formulates it thus: 'The sympathetic system serves the unfolding of actual energy, the parasympathetic the restitution and preservation of potential productivity.'[67] Treichler characterises this polarity in his essay in the following way:

> It should be mentioned that the parasympathetic system, which includes the vagus nerve, serves more the perception of form conditions, while the sympathetic system perceives and communicates the activities of the organs.[68]

This is a formulation that shows the way to the solution of our problem. The formation of theories about the functions of the vegetative nervous system suffers today from a fatal error. Invariably, an active motor effect is ascribed to these nerves and the fact that they are purely sensory, sensing organs is almost entirely overlooked. When Treichler assigns a sensitivity for the life activities of the organs to the sympathetic system, he may well have found the right interpretation of it. The sympathetic system is the organ of the sense of life. But what is meant by the 'perception of form conditions'?[69]

Rudolf Steiner has shown that around the seventh year children experience a decisive metamorphosis of their life forces. Until then they have been devoted almost exclusively to plastically formative activity in the organism, when they were forming the structure and shape of the organs and tissues. But at the time of the second dentition a part of these formative forces is set free and transformed into those forces needed by our thinking for its activity. What Treichler calls 'perception of form conditions', and associates with the vagus nerve, belongs to those plastically formative life forces that are later active as thought forces.

Can we not dare, on the basis of everything we have presented thus far, to assign to the vagus nerve with all its many branches passing through the whole living organism, the role of the organ of the sense of thought? This nerve is indeed the 'physical' part, the part permanently retained in a material way, of all life processes performed in our organism. Just as the sympathetic part of the autonomic nervous system is the organ of the sense of life, so the parasympathetic part, which is connected with the brain via the vagus nerve, is the organ of the sense of thought.[70]

Thus, light is thrown on the phenomenon that was the starting point of our deliberations. The muscles of the larynx, as voluntary organs, are supplied from two pairs of nerves branching off from the trunk of the vagus nerve. Now we come to understand why the sense of thought is formed along with the development of speech during the second year. After children acquire the word sense, they become conscious of the surrounding sphere of language. Until then they perceived words and sentences merely as signs for sounds and noises, but now for the first time they begin to understand what is expressed in the spoken word. Children also begin to imitate the words and sentences they perceive and to use their larynx for the activity of speaking. For it is not the nerve impulses that make use of the larynx as speech organ, but the soul itself preparing to speak. Thereby, the speech organs and their muscles, as well as the corresponding nerves, are permeated by the attempts at sound formation continually being made by children.

The muscles gradually come under the domination of the speaking soul and the word images stream through the corresponding nerves into the whole autonomic nervous system.[71] There they merge with the life activities of the whole organism and imprint it with the characteristics of each child's native language. The human being is deeply influenced in all its life processes by the effects of the language in whose sphere they grow up and live. This comes about along the path we have just described.

The word forms that are counted among the life processes flow in and stream along the path of the nerves. They also work through the vagus nerve with all its ramifications and in this way transform it into an organ that can act as the physical apparatus for the activity of the sense of thought.

The formative forces active in the life processes are identical with those that have built up all living forms in the world. They work in nature as well as in human beings, and thus are part of the eternal ideas that form all life and being. When they meet with the forms of words and sounds, the way leading through the gate of the word is opened to the ideas themselves.

We have called the pyramidal system a musical instrument with many thousands of strings that enable us to perceive speech, and we can call the vagus nerve as form the sum total of all that is active in us as life organism. This realm is the sphere of the creative ideas that hold sway in the living organism, form-creating and form-destroying. We can look upon this life sphere as a mighty brain, not fixed in shape, but being formed ever anew in the stream of life and deeds. The twigs and branches of the vagus nerve rise from it, combine with each other and converge like the twigs and branches in the crown of a tree to form the trunk. But here the trunk rises from below upwards and plunges its roots into the other brain that is enclosed as physical structure in the skull. The vagus nerve passes from the living interplay of the organs into the dead and rigidly formed brain.[72] On this bridge between life and death the organ of the sense of thought is formed ever anew. The ideas and concepts brought to us through the words of other human beings meet in the vagus nerve the living formative forces that are active in our life organism. From this meeting arises the immediate cognition characteristic of all sense processes. It can enter the sphere of consciousness because the vagus nerve has such a close anatomical connection with the brain.[73] Thus, the ideas contained in the word images can be recognised and experienced in our waking consciousness.

These phenomena now make possible a beginning for the understanding of the morphological manifestation that finds its expression in the nerve supply of the larynx. Here the parasympathetic nervous system, to the extent that the vagus nerve is involved in it, is revealed as the sense organ of the sense of thought.[74]

The ego sense

The knowledge gained in the last section of this chapter can be summarised as follows:

1. In the course of their first year children acquire the sense of speech in connection with the ability to walk upright.
2. The sense of speech opens up the sphere of the word and makes possible the development of speech in children's second year.
3. The sense of thought is, in turn, developed in the course of learning to speak.

With the awakening of the sense of thought in their third year, children open themselves to the thoughts communicated to them through the words of other people. As a climax of this development, we discovered that children could refer to themselves by the term 'I', thereby crossing the threshold of the third year.

In a later presentation of his theory of the senses, Rudolf Steiner adds the ego sense to the senses of speech and thought and characterises it in the following way:

> What is important here is not so much knowing about our own ego, but meeting other people who reveal their ego to us. Perception of the other person's ego, not of our own, that is the function of the ego sense.[75]

An especially detailed description of how the ego sense functions was given by Rudolf Steiner at the occasion of the founding of the Waldorf School. There he said:

> If you meet another person, the following occurs: for a short period you perceive a person, and he or she makes an impression upon you. That impression disturbs you inwardly; you feel that the person, a being comparable to yourself, makes an impression upon you like an attack. The result is that you 'defend' yourself inwardly, you resist this attack and become inwardly aggressive towards the person. In this aggression you become crippled, and the aggression ceases. Then the other person can again make an impression upon you, and after you thus have time to regain your aggressive strength, you carry out another act of aggression. This is the relationship that exists when one person meets another and perceives the other I – that is devotion to the other – inner resistance; sympathy–antipathy ...

However, there is still something else. As sympathy develops, you go to sleep in the other person; as antipathy develops, you wake up, and so forth. In the vibrations of meeting another person, there is a rapid alternation between waking and sleeping. We have to thank the organ of the I-sense that this can occur. This organ of I-sensing is so formed that it explores the I of another person, not wakefully but in its sleeping will, and then quickly delivers the results of this sleepy exploration to cognition, that is, to the nervous system.[76]

Here we see clearly the two-phase character of ego perception, which seems to function like an inner breathing process.[77] With this two-phase nature the period in child development can be indicated, at least in passing, during which children begin to unfold their ego sense.[78] During the first two years children primarily react 'sympathetically' towards other people. Especially if they are not spoiled, children are full of confidence towards other people and seldom feel discomfort towards strangers. Infants may often be hesitant when meeting others and may feel fear or anxiety towards strangers, but once they have overcome their shyness, they will throw themselves into the other being, full of sympathy – they 'sleep' into the other one.

Elsa Köhler writes the following about her Annie at the age of two years and six months:

> Annie wants to be sociable. Children of different ages attract her attention. When she sees a child in the street, she stops, runs towards him, gives him her hand and wants to kiss him. Frightened mothers and nurse maids often pull their children away and look unkindly at Annie. She does not feel this mistrust.[79]

In her meeting with other egos, Annie is still entirely clothed in sympathy and does not confront them 'consciously', which means that she has not yet developed the alternation between sympathy and antipathy in the realm of the ego sense.

For this age there hardly exists any difference between human beings, animals and objects. All things in the surrounding world are equal in action as well as in suffering. Thus, Annie can say that her toy rabbit will watch her eating, while the next day it will be the orange that lies on the table that will watch her. Children, therefore, have pity for things as well as people, and a broken biscuit can bring them as easily to tears as a mother who must lie in bed with a headache. I remember a little three-year-old melancholic who, when we all sat at table, suddenly broke into bitter tears. He gradually let us know that it was the chair standing so lonely and unused against the wall that caused him such great misery.

Such behaviour is not connected with the fact that infants treat all things anthropomorphically, as superficial psychology would have it. It is rather the other way around, and everything is felt uniformly without life and soul. It, therefore, can be pitied, feared, mothered, and embraced with sympathy. Wilhelm Hansen[80] quite rightly says:

> A separation between subject and object does not yet exist for the child in the sense that the subject has consciousness through the knowledge of the object from which he differs. From the fact that he applies names used for soul qualities such as thinking, being good, expecting, enjoying, etc., also to his animal, plant and material surroundings, we are justified in drawing only one conclusion: that the child does not yet separate these domains of the world from those of the ensouled human being, nor does he draw a line between different realms

of existence. He thinks and reacts towards everything in the same way.[81]

This illustrates clearly that the ego sense has not yet developed in the infant. Otherwise, they could immediately differentiate between human beings and the other beings and things of its environment. Children embrace everything with a certain amount of sympathy, which means they sleep into things and beings without being able to meet them in the recoil of awakening antipathy. This process of waking up does not occur until about the time of the first period of defiance. Between their third and fourth years, children begin to oppose the surrounding world for the first time, and to put their own will antipathetically over against their environment. Everything that until this point had been easy and possible without fuss, now comes about under difficulty and with arguments. Children want to do everything themselves – to dress and undress by themselves, to decide independently how to play and often to do exactly the opposite of what grown-ups would like them to do. During this time, the first conflicts between children and their parents and siblings occur because they become aware of their own independent being quite differently from before.

The significant meeting, about which we spoke in the third chapter, has taken place. The eternal individuality of the child was called the awakener of the sleeping thinking, and we said: 'In that moment when they behold one another face to face, the consciousness of the individual ego first awakens' (see page 84). This process of becoming conscious is the cause of the first period of defiance.

Remplein describes this stage concretely. He says:

Behind the child's outer rejection of the play community stands an important development of the

ego consciousness ... The ego centre, which hitherto
had only registered all experiences without becoming
conscious of itself, now becomes the object of experience.
At the same time the symbiotic unity of child and world
falls apart and a first separation occurs between ego and
non-ego. This transition happens without deliberation
or self-reflection. In action and in meeting the world the
child becomes conscious of himself.[82]

This process makes it possible for the 'sympathetic'
attitude of children to become ambivalent and for them to
bring distinctly antipathetic features into the fabric of their
experiences. It is not fear, anxiety, shame, or repulsion of
anything alien that puts children into opposition to their
environment. Rather it is the awakening consciousness
of self that leads them into an attitude of defiance. It is a
truly positive phase of development that starts here, and it
should be valued as such by parents and teachers. Children
wake up to the consciousness of their own selves and do
not want to lose this awakening again. Therefore, they
become defiant.

Along with meeting the other with sympathy, the
attitude of defiance enables children to acquire rejection
also because only in the continuous alternation between
these two phases of the soul can the ego sense develop.
This development, however, does not seem to progress as
quickly and as directly as that of the senses of speech and
thought. The ego sense needs a long period of development
for its complete unfolding.

In the third chapter we pointed out the radical difference
between walking and speaking on the one hand and thinking
on the other. In a similar way there also exists a radical
difference between the senses of speech and thought and
the ego sense. Though the awakening thinking is a necessary
presupposition for the gradual development of the ego sense,

this highest sense does not unfold along with the development of thinking in the same way that the senses of speech and thought were formed during the acquisition of the ability to walk upright and of speech. The development of thinking may certainly produce the awakening of the ego consciousness, but this is not the ego sense. Only someone who has gained full consciousness of their own ego can, as a consequence of this, develop an ego sense.

The acquisition of thought may well become the mirror of the ego, in which the latter then begins to experience itself. This self-experience makes possible the antipathetic attitude essential for the forming of the ego sense. The meeting of two ego-conscious beings results in those two phases, the sympathetic as well as the antipathetic impulses, which lead to an immediate experience of the other ego. Up to now, detailed observations in this field of child development hardly exist. One can, however, assume that in shape and appearance, the father is the most important stimulator for the development of the ego sense. He becomes a symbol of the surrounding world that confronts the child, not protecting like the mother, but demanding (please see the accompanying endnote for a more contemporary reading of this point – Ed.).[83]

The formation of the ego sense is not completed until the ninth year. It is consolidated at this threshold of child development and Rudolf Steiner has called particular attention to it. He describes this time of transformation in the following way:

> At the age of nine, the child experiences a truly complete transformation of their being that indicates an important transformation of their soul life as well as their physical experience. At that time, the human being begins to feel separated from their surroundings and learns to differentiate between the world and themselves. If we

can observe accurately, we have to admit that until that transformation, the world and the I are more or less conjoined in human consciousness. Beginning at the age of nine (of course I mean this only approximately), human beings can differentiate between themselves and the world. We must take that into consideration in what and how we teach children starting at the age of nine. Until then, it is best not to confuse them with descriptions and characterisations of things that are separate from the human being, or that we should consider separate from the human being. When we tell a child a story or a fairy tale, we describe the animals and perhaps the plants in the way we would speak about people. In a certain sense, we personify plants and animals. We can justifiably personify them because the child cannot yet differentiate between themselves and the world in a way similar to the way they experience it.[84]

With the ninth year this experience changes radically. The formation of the ego sense is completed and children learn through the experience of this sense to differentiate between human beings and other beings of nature. The age of fairy tales and legends comes to an end. Parents and teachers are observed critically, and the ego begins to measure itself against other egos. The awakening into the sphere of personality has set in. What began with the first age of defiance has now reached its conclusion.

On two occasions Rudolf Steiner spoke about the sense organ underlying the ego sense. One passage reads as follows:

> The organ for perceiving the I spreads over the entire human being and consists of a very subtle substance. For that reason, people do not speak of an organ for perceiving another's I.[85]

In the second passage he speaks much more extensively about this sense organ:

> There is indeed an organ for perceiving an I, just as there are organs for perceiving colours and tones. But the organ for perceiving an I only originates in the head; from there it spreads out into the entire body, in so far as the body is appended to the head, making of the entire body an organ of perception. So the whole perceptible, physical form of a human being really does function as an organ of perception, the organ for perceiving the I of another. In a certain sense you could also say that the head, in so far as the rest of the body is appended to it and in so far as it sends its ability to perceive another I through the whole human being, is the organ for perceiving another's I. The entire, immobile human being is the organ for perceiving an I – the whole of the human form at rest, with the head as a kind of central point. The organ for perceiving another I is thus the largest of our organs of perception; we ourselves, as physical human beings, constitute the largest of our organs of perception.[86]

Little can be added to such a description because it is manifest that the entire human body, 'insofar as the body is appended to the head', is the organ of perception for the ego sense.[87] Until about the ninth year, however, children grow directly through the forces of the head. During infancy the head is still overly large in comparison with the rest of the body and this disproportion is harmonised only gradually, especially between the third and ninth years. The limbs stretch, the trunk of the body grows larger and the head lags behind in growth. As a result, the particularly well-formed body structure arises that children have around the ninth year. From infant form through the first 'change of form' occurring between the seventh and eighth years, that 'shape before puberty' has come about which in its architecture shows such perfect harmony.

The attainment of this shape of the body really depends on the head, whose growth stands in closest connection with the function of two inner secretory glands of the brain, the pineal gland or epiphysis, and the pituitary gland or hypophysis.[88] The working together of these two glands regulates the forces of growth and form in such a way that they lead to a harmonious or disharmonious development of the body. The equilibrium between epiphysis and hypophysis results in the harmonious shape of the body that develops between the seventh and eighth years. Before this time the activity of the epiphysis predominates, later that of the hypophysis. The development of this perfect bodily form, which is corrupted only later in puberty, coincides with the attainment of the ego sense. During this stage, human beings have reached the highest level of their physical development. They have become the true image of the human being who have also unfolded the highest sense, the ego sense. In a certain sense, this is also the beginning of a descent because, during pre-puberty and maturity, the body and limbs become earthbound and lose that touch for the other world that they still retained until about the ninth year. Growing human beings fall prey to the earth, become heavy, burdened, and worried about their path of destiny.

Human beings have, however, gained the ego sense, and this they are allowed to keep and carry with them as a lifelong gift from this time onward. The senses of speech and thought likewise remain with them as gifts through which they can approach the spirit of all existence. Through the sense of speech, all treasures of the word are opened. Through the sense of thought, the wisdom of all past and present creation is unveiled. Through the sense of ego, other human beings are recognised as brothers and sisters. Thus, childhood has endowed us with a possession never to be lost.

Walking, speaking, and thinking have made us human. They have raised us from creatures to beings who can recognise themselves. The senses of speech, thought, and ego on the other hand help us to approach the spirit depths of all existence. They open paths into higher worlds that lie beyond the world of the senses. In those three highest senses, the sphere of the senses begins to abolish itself and points the way to its own overcoming. This is a sacrifice because it leads to annihilation. Further on, a resurrection is waiting. The sense world will break asunder and a spirit world will open up beyond.[89]

Our life with courage ending
Eternal life draws near,
With inner glow expanding
Transfigured sense grows clear.

The star world now is flowing
As living golden wine,
Its joys on us bestowing,
Ourselves as stars shall shine[90]

Novalis[91]

Endnotes

In the following notes, König's comments are marked with (KK) and those marked (Ed.) are the editor's. References to the work of Rudolf Steiner include volume numbers either for the Collected Works (CW) or the German Gesamtausgabe (GA).

Introduction

1. This first sentence introduces the fundamental ontological and anthropological perspective from which König approaches his study of child development. This perspective is grounded in Rudolf Steiner's Anthroposophy, a view of the human being as a spiritual individuality that exists prior to conception and birth, enters an embodied experience of the world through the processes of conception, birth and human development, and then reverts back to an unembodied way of being, taking with them the essence of the encounters, experiences and relationships developed during earthly life as a source of further growth and development. (Ed.)

2. König is referring here to an expanded understanding of perception and sensory physiology developed initially by Rudolf Steiner and elaborated, among others, by König himself (see especially König, K. (2006). *A Living Physiology.* Camphill Books; and König, K. (2021). *Die Zwölf Sinne des Menschen: Band 1 and 2* (The Twelve Senses of Man: Volumes 1 and 2). Freies Geistesleben, Stuttgart.) (Ed.)

Chapter 1. Acquiring the Ability to Walk Upright

1. Though König does not reference him here, his perspective on the question of movement control resonates with the work of Soviet neuropsychologist Nikolai A. Bernstein (1896–1966). Central to this perspective is the recognition that motor control cannot be explained as the result of learning fixed patterns of muscle activation directed by the central nervous system (CNS). In fact, any movement sequence

can be brought about through an infinite number of different patterns of activity in the various muscle groups involved. Conversely, the same pattern of activity will lead to a different resulting movement if, for example, the position of the mover in relation to gravity is altered even slightly. Consequently, the role of the CNS in motor control and integration must be understood as primarily sensory: the mover constantly perceives and monitors their own movement in relation to the target object and environment, and muscular activity is adjusted organically during its flow. For this intentional movement to be successful, therefore, two things are key: (1) the absence of fixed, centrally controlled patterns of activation (e.g., reflexes), and (2) a well-developed capacity of motor proprioception. Bernstein's work only became increasingly well-known in the West well after his death. Even though is he considered the founding father of modern kinesiology and biomechanics, one of his foundational works was only translated into English as recently as 2021 (Latash, M.L. (ed.) (2020). *Bernstein's Construction of Movements: The Original Text and Commentaries.* Routledge). It would be fruitful to revisit this chapter from a contemporary perspective in connection with Rudolf Steiner's comments about motor nerves on the one hand, and the current state of understanding of motor control in the Bernsteinian tradition on the other. (Ed.)

2.   While it is not apparent that König was aware of the work of Bernstein, his main point of reference appears to be the work of the early-twentieth-century Dutch physiologists Magnus and de Kleijn. While having made valuable contributions to the understanding of the primitive reflexes, their work represents the older and more reductionist tradition in the neurosciences that both Bernstein and König criticise from their respective holistic standpoints. A take-home message from this historical development is that a paradigm that looks at movement control as originating in the CNS, in the form of fixed patterns of activation, provides a fairly good framework for understanding primitive reflexes, but is completely inadequate for an understanding of the control of free intentional movement. The latter needs to be approached from an Bernsteinian or ecological perspective (i.e., as in some significant sense initiated from, and directed towards, its object or task in the periphery). (Ed.)

3.   William Stern (1871–1938) was one of the pioneers of empirical-scientific psychology. Besides child psychology, he also contributed significantly to the development of the concept of an 'intelligence quotient' (IQ). Unlike other major proponents of IQ, however, he remained cautious about its use as the central measure of 'intelligence'. While König is appreciative here of Stern's

investigations of child development, elsewhere, he firmly rejects the reductive measurement of intelligence in terms of IQ and, in particular, the instrumentalisation of IQ for eugenic purposes (see König, K. (2009). *The Child with Special Needs: Letters and Essays on Curative Education*. Floris.). (Ed.)

4. Stern, *Psychology of Early Childhood*, p. 69. (KK)

5. Rudolf Magnus (1873–1927), German pharmacologist and physiologist. Adriaan de Kleijn (1883–1949), Dutch medical scientist. (Ed.)

6. Magnus, Rudolf and de Kleijn, Adriaan, 'Körperstellung, Gleichgewicht und Bewegung' (Body Position, Balance and Movement). (KK)

7. König takes the step here, which is fundamental to his approach in this chapter, of considering how each step in motor integration is accompanied by a corresponding shift in a child's consciousness, in their awareness of self and world. In doing this, König anticipates more recent attempts to understand consciousness and cognition as grounded in the whole body (and not just the brain, for example). A foundational text for this line of research, which integrates neuroscience, phenomenology, and psychology, is Varela, F.J., Thompson, E. & Rosch, E. (2017), *The Embodied Mind: Cognitive Science and Human Experience* (Revised Edition), MIT Press (first published in 1991). It would be fruitful to re-examine the themes König presents here through the lens of the contemporary research on 'embodied cognition' that follows this framework. (Ed.)

8. Adalbert Stifter (1805–68). Austrian writer, painter and educator. While having had a significant impact in German literature, he remains largely unknown outside of the German-speaking context. (Ed.)

9. Stifter, *Betrachtungen und Bilder* (Reflections and Images). (KK)

10. Here, König identifies the feedback loop between movement and sensory experience as the driver of development of both sensory and motor integration. This develops hand in hand through the activity of children, which is initiated through their relation to, interest in and orientation towards their environment. (Ed.)

11. Stern, *Psychology of Early Childhood*, p. 124. (KK)

12. This exposition by König has affinities with another classic of psychology first published in 1979, J.J. Gibson's *Ecological Approach to Visual Perception* (Taylor & Francis (2015)). Gibson situates visual perception within the context of a being that looks around and actively moves through their special environment. Seeing, according to Gibson, cannot be understood as an internal process

of 'sensory processing' between the eye and the brain, but takes place between a mover and the visual environment, with all the opportunities for action that this environment affords. Again, it would be interesting to take König's approach further in dialogue with the body of research that has followed from Gibson's seminal work. (Ed.)

13. Adolf Portmann (1897–1982). Swiss biologist, zoologist, anthropologist, and natural philosopher. He coined the term 'physiologische Frühgeburt', characterising the newborn human being as a 'premature baby' in comparison to animals, whose development is typically much more functionally mature at the moment of birth. According to Portmann, the human need to complete important steps belonging to 'fetal' development outside the womb opens the human being up to the influence of cultural and social forces in a unique way not found in animals. (Ed.)

14. Portmann, *Biologische Fragmente* (Biological Fragments). (KK)

15. Fritz Stirinmann (1877–1947). Swiss pediatrician and author of a well-known text on early childhood development, *Psychologie des neugeborenen Kindes* (Psychology of the Newborn Child), first published in 1940. (Ed.)

16. Brock, J, *Biologische Daten für Kinderarzt* (Biological Data for Pediatricians), volume 2, Berlin 1934

17. Otto Storch (1886–1951). Austrian biologist and zoologist. In his 1947 book *Die Sonderstellung des Menschen in Lebensabspiel und Vererbung* (The Special Position of the Human Being with Regard to the Course of Life and in Hereditary Processes), he tries to characterise from a biological point of view what distinguishes the human being from (other) animals. One aspect of this, according to Storch, lies in the much greater role of learned, as opposed to inherited or congenital, motor patterns. (Ed.)

18. Storch, *Die Sonderstellung des Menschen* (The Special Position of the Human Being). (KK)

19. Otfried Förster (1873–1941). German neurosurgeon and pioneer of neuroscience. He conducted foundational research on the role of the spinal reflexes in spasticity, the involvement of the cerebral cortex in motor coordination, and on epilepsy. (Ed.)

20. Cécile Vogt (née Mugnier, 1875–1962) and Oskar Vogt (1870–1959). Pioneers of neuroscientific research and co-founders of neurological research centres in Berlin, Moscow and Neustadt (Schwarzwald), the latter now known as the Cécile & Oskar Vogt Institute for Brain Research at the University of Düsseldorf. The Vogt-Vogt syndrome, a neurological disorder appearing in early childhood and leading to double-sided athetosis, is named after them. (Ed.)

21. Athetosis is a symptom characterised by involuntary writhing movements of the limbs and sometimes also the neck and tongue. It typically occurs in conjunction with damage to specific areas of the brain resulting from birth complications, and often co-occurs with cerebral palsy. (Ed.)

22. R. Hassler, 'Extrapyramidal-motorische Syndrome und Erkrankungen' (Extrapyramidal motor syndromes and disordes), in *Neurologie. Handbuch der Inneren Medizin*, volume 5 / 0, Berlin, Heidelberg 1953. (Ed.)

23. The term 'chorea' (from the ancient Greek for 'dance') describes disordered involuntary movements of the limbs that are often accompanied by athetosis and are associated with various neurological disorders. (Ed.)

24. Little's disease, also known as spastic diplegia, is a form of cerebral palsy manifesting constant tightness and stiffness of the muscles of both legs. *Pes equinus* (literally, horse foot) is a condition in which the heel of the foot cannot be lowered to the ground. It is a common symptom of cerebral palsy. (Ed.)

25. An inability to gain voluntary control of movement (ataxia), which has its origins in damage to the cerebellum, a part of the brain that is central to motor learning and the control of voluntary movements. (Ed.)

26. König writes here from a perspective that acknowledges a close interrelationship between motor development on the one hand and psychological and cognitive development on the other. Research on these interrelationships has developed significantly in the years since his writing, but remains in the early stages, with a need for further and more specific exploration. However, several recent studies have shown and/or explored evidence related to the interrelationships explored here by König. Examples are: Diamond, A. (2000). 'Close interrelationship of motor development and cognitive development and of the cerebellum and prefrontal cortex'. *Child Development*, 2000 Jan–Feb; 71(1): 44–56. Steinlin, M. (2008). 'Cerebellar disorders in childhood: cognitive problems', *Cerebellum* 2008; 7(4): 607–10. Baillieux, H. et al. (2008). 'Cerebellar neurocognition: insights into the bottom of the brain'. *Clin Neurol Neurosurg*, 2008 Sep; 110(8): 763–73. Jylänki et al. (2022). 'Cognitive and Academic Outcomes of Fundamental Motor Skill and Physical Activity Interventions Designed for Children with Special Educational Needs: A Systematic Review'. *Brain Science* 2022 Jul 28; 12(8): 1001. Bailleux et al. (2008) affirm that 'The traditional view on the core functions of the cerebellum consists of the regulation of motor coordination, balance and motor speech. However, during

the past decades results from neuroanatomical, neuroimaging and clinical studies have substantially extended the functional role of the cerebellum to cognitive and affective regulation' (abstract). This clearly is another area for fruitful further exploration, bridging emerging neuroscientific perspectives with König's and Steiner's anthroposophical spiritual-scientific framework (see also Jylänki et al. 2022). (Ed.)

27. König's comments regarding school readiness should be understood as referring to schooling in the traditional sense, as significantly focused on the acquisition of skills such as reading, writing and arithmetic. If the task of school is understood more broadly as the creation of an environment and processes in which children of all abilities can learn and grow together in accordance with their individual needs and capacities, the perspective on child development developed here should not be seen as standing in contradiction with contemporary concepts of inclusive education. König's comments should certainly not be read as advocating the exclusion of children with complex developmental needs from education, but rather as highlighting that for some children, foundational embodied developmental processes need to stand in the foreground and take precedence over 'classic' academic schooling and learning for the educational process to be individually and developmentally appropriate. (Ed.)

28. Portmann, *Biologische Fragmente* (Biological Fragments), p. 72. (KK)

29. In other words, with the acquisition of upright walking, a child has 'extracted' their entire body from the early and primitive processes of involuntary movement and integrated the entire bodily gestalt into the systems and processes that govern the organisation of voluntary, free and intentional movement within surrounding three-dimensional space and the gravitational force field. To support these developmental processes from an educational or therapeutic perspective, we do not need to fully understand all the complex neurological factors involved but can work on the basis of an observation and understanding of the movement dynamics expressed in space themselves. (Ed.)

30. König now shifts from a more analytical account of motor development to an imaginative integration of the whole process to grasp its inherent dynamic gesture. In trying to apprehend the organising principle in this organic process of transformation, König identifies this principle as that which Steiner describes from many different perspectives as the human 'I': the spiritual individuality that exists prior to conception and birth and enters through the body into a relationship with the external world of

space through the processes of sensory-motor development explored here. In ancient mythologies and ceremonial contexts, this principle has often been imagined as, and symbolised by, the staff – whether, for example, it be the staff of the shepherd, of the king, of the bishop or the Staff of Hermes/Mercury. König alludes here to these symbols and images. (Ed.)

31. Here, König undertakes a further imaginative step, with imagination understood as a cognitive process that can take hold of and give expression to holistic and organic processes and phenomena that defy analytic and linear explanation. The picture developed here can be understood as a meditation on the resonance between the inherent rhythms and time structure of the 'microcosmic' developmental processes described, and the 'macrocosmic' rhythms that give a time signature to the external spatial world with which children enter into a conscious and eventually self-aware relationship through these embodied processes. (Ed.).

32. Steiner, *Spiritual Guidance of the Individual and Humanity*, p. 6. (KK)

33. Steiner, *The Karma of Untruthfulness: Volume 1* (CW173). See lecture of December 21, 1916. (KK)

34. While it may be difficult to verify or falsify the accuracy of the specific assertions made here through the historic record, the general idea that in the more ancient human past, human reproduction was aligned with the cycle of the year is not so far-fetched. In fact, there is contemporary research that indicates that there are both measurable natural (e.g., climatic) and cultural seasonal effects on the variable frequency of conception throughout the year. Simó-Noguera et al. (2020) show that in Catholic Spain of the early twentieth century, before the influence of the Catholic church began to wane, conceptions were drastically reduced during Lent (the time of fasting preceding Easter), with a significant 'rebound' immediately after Lent, in the days and weeks after the March equinox. This led to an accumulation of births nine months later, during late December and January, exactly as suggested here. (See Simó-Noguera et al. (2020). 'Lent impact on the seasonality of conceptions during the twentieth century in Spain'. *Eur J Popul.* 2020 Nov; 36(5): 875–93.) If, as the authors suggest, in the past natural and cultic seasonal rhythms were often strongly aligned with each other and had a much stronger ordering influence on daily life than in modern societies, and if the processes of reproduction were considered among the most sacred, and therefore most subject to cultic ordering, it is not inconceivable that something like the situation described above could have been a historical reality. At the very least, this framing makes the idea of imagining the process of

human reproduction (and by extension of early child development) as mapped onto the rhythms of the year meaningful and potentially insightful. Interestingly, in modern societies, seasonality has been shown to result in exactly the opposite pattern, with increased conception in late autumn and births in midsummer (Gudziunaite, S. and Moshammer, H. (2022). 'Temporal patterns of weekly births and conceptions predicted by meteorology, seasonal variation, and lunar phases'. *Wien Klin Wochenschr.* 2022 Jul; 134(13–14): 538–45.) and to be strongly influenced by socio-demographic factors (Bobak, M. and Gjonca, A. (2001). 'The seasonality of life birth is strongly influenced by socio-demographic factors'. *Hum Reprod.* 2001 Jul; 16(7): 1512–17.) This is clearly another area for fruitful further historical, cultural, anthropological and biomedical research. (Ed.)

35. In this final passage of the chapter, König brings the steps of his spiritual-scientific method to completion. He began with a review of the state of knowledge of (at the time) current empirical and analytical science regarding early motor development, then integrated the emerging picture into a holistic phenomenology of the process. This phenomenology was then transformed into an imaginative picture that, at the same time, allowed an artistic sense for the time structure of the process to arise. Now, König shifts towards the impulse for action, the 'new power to help' that can arise from this newly integrated, imaginatively, and contemplatively deepened understanding of the essential process involved in learning to walk. If held inwardly in the right way, this understanding can – so König's implicit claim – become a source of a new and heightened capacity to support others in their development. This is not so much because general 'recipes' or 'guidelines' for pedagogical or therapeutic action can be deduced from this understanding, but rather because the educator or therapist who has internalised the dynamics of this process becomes able to 'read' complex individual developmental situations in a new way and draw out of them, in the encounter between 'I' and 'I', new ideas and creative intuitions for the pedagogical and therapeutic action needed in each unique situation. For König, for whom the healing deeds of Christ described in the Gospels provide an essential spiritual point of reference, this capacity for healing deeds is encapsulated in the scene he references. In John 5:1–18, Christ meets a lame man at the pool of Bethesda who is unable to access its healing waters because of his inability to walk. Through the words spoken to him by Christ, according to König's interpretation here, the I, the spiritual individuality, the 'sun power', is invited, drawn out to complete what has remained incomplete, to enter through the bodily gestalt into the surrounding world and thereby lift the body out of the forces of gravity into uprightness.

The man no longer needs the water in the pond but can walk freely. What has been developed here can provide an inner foundation from which the educator or therapist can offer a similar effective invitation to others and discover how to do so in each individual case – according to König's suggestion. (Ed.)

Chapter 2. Learning Our Native Language

1. Portmann, *Biologische Fragmente* (Biological Fragments), p. 74. The point made here by Portmann was affirmed in the work of Noam Chomsky on language acquisition, especially in his 1965 foundational text *Aspects of the Theory of Syntax* (MIT Press). The body of research by Chomsky and others that followed its publication led to the development of the 'generative grammar' framework to the study of language and its various spin offs, including the contemporary 'minimalist program'. While there are significant technical differences between language acquisition models in this 'family' of theories, they all recognise that language is a rule-based system with an underlying 'Universal Grammar' of which the grammars of particular languages are narrower variants, and that because of this, language is generative, meaning that even though each language consists of a limited set of symbols, the grammar allows for infinite possibilities of generating utterances that can be understood by others who have mastered the same language, even if the utterance has never been spoken or heard before. This syntax-based generativity is not found in animal communication. It also means that it is impossible to explain language acquisition by reference to either fixed congenital communication patterns or to the kinds of learning principles described by behaviourist learning theory, which govern most of animal learning. In this sense, also, sign languages are full, generative human languages with a syntax of their own. They merely use a different medium of expression in mimicry and gesture, rather than the production of speech. For the same reasons, Chomsky has also expressed scepticism that evolutionary theory in its current form will be able to explain the emergence of language (for an accessible discussion, see Chomsky, N. and Moro, A. (2022). *The Secrets of Words*. MIT Press.). In spite of the logical difficulty of explaining the emergence of syntax-based language from forms of communication that lack generative syntax by means of the evolutionary and learning mechanisms recognised in the materialist-reductionist framework, most scholars in this tradition assume that, eventually, such an explanation will be available. Notable among them is Steven Pinker who, in his 1994 classic *The Language Instinct* (William Morrow & Co.), argues that the 'Universal Grammar' is

grounded on a set of brain structures that have evolved through natural selection, thereby claiming to have shown how to overcome the logical reasons for Chomsky's scepticism on the matter. As will be apparent, König does not locate the universal essence of language in a material and evolutionarily contingent aspect of brain architecture shared by all humans, but, following Steiner, in the primal spiritual essence of language itself, as something that has being in its own right, with which the human being can enter into an intimate and generative relationship (including by means of social processes and physical organs that support this relationship), but which also always transcends the individual human being. It could be fruitful to attempt a reading of contemporary research on language in the Chomskyan tradition through a non-materialist and non-reductionist lens and to bring König's perspective on language and language acquisition into dialogue with that. (Ed.)

2. König uses the German term 'Sprache'. It is important to note that 'Sprache' can be translated either as 'language' or as 'speech'. The translator chose 'speech', presumably to highlight the productive aspect of language as a human activity. However, readers of the English translation should consider both aspects, 'speech' and 'language', wherever the term 'speech' appears in this chapter. This will become important, especially when considering the ontological status that König gives speech/language as an entity with its own essence and lawfulness, which in some significant sense transcends and precedes individual human speech activity. This transpersonal aspect may be better captured in the English term 'language'. (Ed.)

3. While in the first chapter König proceeded from an account of scientific findings to an imaginative picture, here he already calls up one of the world's great creation myths to shed light on key aspects of speech and language – namely, that on the one hand, the capacity to name things separates the human being from the world and establishes the subject-object divide, the I-it divide, which constitutes human (as opposed to animal) consciousness, and that on the other hand, language connects when it lives in the space between two interlocuters, between I and you. In fact, it needs the space between I and you to become fully manifest in its true being. This line of contemplation is perhaps most fully developed in the work of Martin Buber (1878–1965), particularly in his 1923 essay 'I and Thou'. (Ed.)

4. Here, König invokes the non-materialist view, discussed earlier, that language should be thought of as something that has a reality and essence in its own right that precedes the phylogenetic and/ or ontogenetic development of the neurological and other structures in human beings that are needed for mastery of language

acquisition. In fact, the development of these structures is in both cases a consequence of the gradual acquisition and use of language by human beings, not its antecedent. This view is consistent with the observation of a critical period in language acquisition after which, if a child has not developed a primary language, those structures that can only be built through the acquisition of language from the environment and its gradual mastery, can no longer be fully formed, as the window of plasticity has closed without their establishment. Conversely, if these structures have been established through the use of one primary language, they can serve as foundations for the later acquisition (albeit often with diminishing ease) of other languages built on the same universal principles. (Ed.)

5. Steiner, *Transforming the Soul: Volume 2*, lecture of January 20, 1910, pp.12f. (KK)

6. So far, König has simply given an account of the key organs involved in the production of speech, albeit already with some imaginative elements. In the following, he builds this image once more, but this time shifting attention to the dynamic, processual interrelationships between the different organs and functions as they play upon each other with their respective processes. The imaginative elements in this account serve to evoke a qualitative sense for these processes, like the functional components of a complex musical instrument. This is another example of König's method of an imaginative phenomenology. (Ed.)

7. From this, it is also clear that any disturbance in the integration of movement and establishment of motor control will have an effect on the acquisition and production of speech, which is itself a refined and internalised motor process that has become the instrument of language. This is also the case with sign language, where more outward oriented aspects of the motor system take on that role. (Ed.)

8. Arnold Gehlen (1904–76) described the human being as a being that is incomplete (in contrast to the animals). This incompleteness creates a vulnerability that is compensated through the creation of culture and cultural institutions, which are needed to stabilise human existence. Language, as a 'magical technique' alongside science and art, is one of the vehicles for this. For more on Gehlen's complex and at times problematic contribution, see Magerski, C. (2021). (Ed.). *Die Macht der Institution: Zum Staatsverständnis Arnold Gehlens* (The Power of the Institution: Arnold Gehlen's Understanding of the State). Nomos. (Ed.)

9. Karl Bühler (1879–1963). German psychologist and linguist. Bühler's theory of language was one of the most influential approaches to

the study of language in the twentieth century. The three aspects of speech that König characterises earlier in this chapter appear to be based on Bühler's so-called 'organon model' of language, in which he distinguishes an expressive, a representational and an appellative, or communicative, function of speech. See Bühler, K. (1934). *Sprachtheorie* (Language Theory). Fischer. (Ed.)

10. Gehlen, *Der Mensch: Seine Natur und seine Stellung in der Welt* (Man: His Nature and Place in the World), p. 208. (KK)

11. A reminder, here, to consider the term 'language' as an alternate translation for König's German term 'Sprache'. (Ed.)

12. Otto Jespersen (1860–1943). Danish linguist. Researched syntax and language development. (Ed.)

13. The question, to what extent language precedes thinking and shapes our experience and our conceptual grasp of the world – the extent to which we experience and understand the world *through* language – has been a subject of scientific investigation and debate in a modern sense at least since the European Enlightenment. One of the strongest formulations of 'linguistic determinism' – the view that the particular structure of a person's language determines their way of seeing and thinking about the world – is known as the 'Sapir-Whorf hypothesis', after linguists Edward Sapir (1884–1939) and Benjamin Whorf (1897–1941). It stands in contrast with more universalist views of language, such as those following Noam Chomsky (discussed earlier), which emphasise the universally shared deep structural properties of all human languages, and see the variations between languages, though real and significant, as more superficial aspects: they might be expected to colour cognition, but not ultimately cause any real divergence in the deep structure of thinking between users of different languages. Today, the Sapir-Whorf hypothesis in its strong form has been largely abandoned. Most researchers regard language and thought as two processes that are distinct but intimately related in ways that need to be explored and understood in a nuanced and carefully differentiated way. This general perspective is consistent with the one embraced by König in this chapter, as will become more apparent through his treatment of cognitive development in the one that follows. For contemporary research on this issue, see especially the work of the Max Planck Institute for Psycholinguistics (https://www.mpi.nl/research). A good entry point into this discussion is Levinson, S. C. (2019). 'Interactional foundations of language: The interaction engine hypothesis', in P. Hagoort (Ed.), *Human Language: From Genes and Brain to Behavior*, MIT Press, pp. 189–200. In contrast to Chomsky, Levinson sees little evidence for a universal deep syntactic structure of language itself but locates the universal aspects of human language use in the universal structure

of human-to-human interaction and communication. (Ed.)

14. See also below, Chapter 3, note 18, for the quotation of Rudolf Steiner. (KK)

15. Or 'language'. (Ed.)

16. Here, again, König moves from a more analytic account based on the state of empirical research to an attempt to distil and grasp the whole gestalt of the process through his imaginative phenomenology. (Ed.)

17. This is a reference to the three elements of Bühler's 'organon model', already mentioned earlier. (Ed.)

18. Bühler, *The Mental Development of the Child*. (KK)

19. Or 'language'. (Ed.)

20. Friedrich Kainz (1897–1977). Austrian philosopher and psychologist of language. Developed a universalist view of language. (Ed.)

21. Kainz, *Psychologie der Sprache: Band 2* (Psychology of Language: Volume 2), p. 3. (KK)

22. Walter Porzig (1895–1961). German linguist. (Ed.)

23. Porzig, *Das Wunder der Sprache* (The Miracle of Language), p. 54. (KK)

24. There is now considerably more research on the question of when language differentiation in babbling begins, including in children raised bilingually. However, the general consensus still holds: babbling begins as motor play activity and the sequence in which different sounds appear is universal as it primarily reflects maturational processes connected with motor control, rather than the sounds of the language spoken in a child's environment. At some point towards the later part of the first year, babbling becomes more imitative and attuned to the native language. This leads to the strengthening of sounds that are used in the native language and the fading of sounds that are not heard in use. For a recent study on this subject, see Best, C.T. et al. (2016). 'Articulating what infants attune to in native speech'. *Ecol Psychol*. 2016 Oct 1; 28(4): 216–61. (Ed.)

25. Kainz, *Psychologie der Sprache: Band 2* (Psychology of Language: Volume 2), p. 4. (KK)

26. Additionally, it is now known that language acquisition of deaf children who grow up in a context where natural sign language is available, mirrors the same time pattern as spoken language acquisition in developing children who can hear. This includes a phase of 'manual babbling', in which both deaf and hearing children engage in gestural motor play. In children exposed to a sign language environment, this manual babbling becomes imitative and attunes to the native sign language in much the same way as vocal babbling

does in relation to the native spoken language. See Lillo-Martin, D. & Henner, J. (2021). 'Acquisition of sign languages'. *Annu Rev Linguist.* 2021 Jan; 7: 395–419. (Ed.).

27. That is, it is no longer just motor play and has become attuned to the native language spoken around the child. (Ed.)

28. Stern, *Psychology of Early Childhood.* (KK)

29. While it is generally agreed that all languages have nouns (naming objects or entities) and verbs (naming actions or processes), adjectives as a distinct word class may not exist universally. In some languages, property words take the same grammatical form as verbs, invoking properties as an activity of the object (e.g., instead of 'The house is big', 'The house "is-being-big"'). In other languages, properties might be expressed in the grammatical form of nouns, which are possessed by the main object or attached to it (e.g., instead of 'The red apple', 'The apple with redness'). There is now an increasing body of literature that explores how language acquisition occurs under these different conditions. Thus, while the pathway that König outlines here holds true in broad brushstrokes, especially for languages that follow the noun-verb-adjective structure, the specifics will vary when the grammatical building blocks of sentences are different. See Dixon, R.M.W. & Aikhenvald, A.Y. (Eds.). (2004). *Adjective Classes: A Cross-linguistic Typology.* Oxford University Press. (Ed.)

30. Stern, *Psychology of Early Childhood.* (KK)

31. Here, again, König engages in his imaginative phenomenology and links the three principal word classes with the threefold organisation of the human gestalt (also central to Steiner's spiritual-scientific view of the human being): the head, which is the focal point of consciousness and still centre from which the world is contemplated, with the 'static' quality of the noun; the limbs with the moving element of action expressed in the verb; and the adjective, which expresses qualities and relationships, with the middle part of the human being, in which the main rhythmical and relational processes of breathing and pulse reside, and which can be experienced as the place where feelings find their embodied resonance. Each sentence, therefore, can be imaginatively seen as a complete threefold 'being' in its own right, which the speaker brings into being and releases into the world. (Ed.)

32. Hans Georg Conon von der Gabelentz (1840–93). (Ed)

33. Stern, *Psychology of Early Childhood,* p. 141. (KK)

34. Kainz, *Psychologie der Sprache: Band 2* (Psychology of Language: Volume 2), p. 35. (KK)

35. Again, the specifics of this process will depend to some degree with the structural properties of the language being acquired. (Ed.)

36. Here, König refers back to ideas that can be found in the work of Gehlen (see earlier), who understands the 'magical technique' of language as precondition and foundation of the state, as an institution needed to 'stabilise' human social existence. It might be better, here, to speak of 'native language community' instead of country. Certainly, it is clear from his other writings, that König was not a proponent of the nineteenth century idea of the nation state that is built on the ideal of a state entity whose boundaries precisely encompass a unified linguistic-cultural community. Recognising the cultural importance of language communities, but understanding them as distinct from questions of statehood and boundaries of territorial governance, allows for the recognition of the dynamic reality of co-existing, overlapping and interpenetrating linguistic communities with fluid and shifting boundaries, including such native language communities within communities as the various sign language communities, which develop their own (sub-) cultural identities. (Ed.)

37. As before, König now offers an imaginative picture of the process he has described so far by invoking the mythical story of the Great Flood, Noah and the Ark from the Book of Genesis (6:9–9:17). The ability to name the world allows children to separate out those experiences they have the power to name from the overwhelming flood of experience and make them their own. This is a precondition for the kind of sense-making that becomes possible through thinking, which penetrates the experience with conceptual understanding. (Ed.)

38. Also often referred to as the 'sense of word'. In his view of the senses (referred to earlier), Steiner (and with him König) distinguishes the capacity to perceive language from the 'sense of hearing', which is concerned with the perception of sound. Though not typically referred to as a 'sense organ', the identification of a distinct perceptual system for the perception of language (as opposed to the hearing of sounds) is uncontroversial. It follows, among other things, from the phenomenon of auditory verbal agnosia (also called 'pure word deafness'), in which hearing is intact, but spoken words can no longer be recognised as such. Instead, they are perceived through the auditory system as mere sounds. In Steiner's and König's terms, this can be understood as a breakdown of the 'sense of speech/word'. Conversely, in (nonverbal) auditory agnosia, the neurological part of the 'sense of hearing', and with it the perception of sounds, is severely impaired, while recognition and comprehension of words as such may remain relatively intact. (Ed.)

39. The function of 'naming' can also break down separately from other productive language functions, as in Wernicke's aphasia, where individuals with damage to the posterior superior temporal gyrus ('Wernicke's area'), just behind the primary auditory cortex in the left hemisphere of the brain, continue to produce syntactically correct and even complex sentences, which are, however, completely meaningless. The areas believed to be involved in damage leading to auditory verbal agnosia are intimately connected with Wernicke's area, and most people with Wernicke's aphasia also show difficulties in receptive speech comprehension, though the two disorders and the precise systems involved are distinct. (Ed.)

40. Steiner, *Transforming the Soul: Volume 2*, p. 18. (KK)

41. In Steiner's and König's view, speech/language is a creative and formative force. This resonates in many contemplative and mythological traditions, including in the Prologue to the Gospel of John, which the quote chosen by König to end this chapter alludes to. Here, König evokes the Logos, the creative power from which the forms of the world derive, as the divine origin and essence of language, which is reflected in human language as it is spoken on Earth, and which gives to it the power to grasp something of the essence of the things and processes of the world. (Ed.)

42. Hamann, *Des Ritters von Rosencreuz letzte Willensmeinung* (Last Opinion of the Knight Rosencreuz). (KK)

Chapter 3. The Awakening of Thinking

1. A current discussion of the interconnectedness of the acquisition of walking, speaking and thinking in early child development, as well as the interrelationships between these functions in rehabilitation processes, can be found in Leisman, G., Moustafa, A.A. & Shafir, T. (2016). 'Thinking, walking, talking: integratory motor and cognitive brain function'. Front Public Health. 2016; 4: 94. (www.ncbi.nlm.nih.gov/pmc/articles/PMC4879139/). The authors emphasise the uniqueness of constant bipedalism with an upright spine in humans and see the 'unique ability to harness gravitational forces as a direct result of the existence of the upright position', which in turn 'has allowed us to develop the binding of the motor system into synchronous, rhythmic, purposeful movement, which expanded to eventually allow for cognitive binding and consciousness.' This specifically human form of motor integration, culminating in upright mastery of gravitational forces, is foundational to the development of self-awareness and higher order cognition and attentional control. A recent study of preschool children with Dravet syndrome (a genetic disorder

causing severe epilepsy in infancy) provides an empirical example of the close relationship between the development of upright walking and cognitive development (Verheyen, K. et al. (2021). 'Independent walking and cognitive development in preschool children with Dravet syndrome'. *Dev Med Child Neurol.* 2021 Apr; 63(4):472–79). (Ed.)

2. A good entry point into current neuroscientific research on the prerequisites for cognition, in line with König's suggestions here, can be found in the work of the Buzsáki Lab at the NYU Neuroscience Institute (https://buzsakilab.com/) and of the Temporal Dynamics of Learning Center at the University of California San Diego (https://tdlc.ucsd.edu/). Buzsáki and colleagues assert that cognition originates in outer action, which is then internalised. Fundamental to their understanding is that 'cognition depends on internal models of the animal and its world, where internally generated sequences can serve to perform "what if" scenarios and anticipate the possible consequences of alternative actions without actually testing them, and aid in the decisions of overt actions' (Buzsáki, G., Peyrache, A. and Kubie, J. (2014). 'Emergence of cognition from action'. *Cold Spring Harbor Symposia on Quantitative Biology, Volume LXXIX*). A good orientation to the complex and interconnected role that space, time and memory play in the emergence of cognition can be found in Buzsáki, G. and Llinás, R. (2017). 'Space and time in the brain'. *Science* 358 (6362), 482–85. Here, they also discuss the role of cultural-linguistic factors, and in particular the influence of different languages, with their different ways of grammatically addressing the dimension of time and sequence, on the cognition of time and process. They also emphasise the role of the hippocampus as a brain structure, in which processes related to the awareness space, time and episodic memory (what König will later call 'time memory') are intimately interconnected (Buzsáki, G. and Tingley, D. (2018). 'Space and time: the hippocampus as a sequence generator'. *Trends in Cognitive Sciences*, October 2018, Volume 22, No. 10, 653–869). See also Buzsáki, G., MacKenzie, S. and Davachi, L. (2022). 'Neurophysiology of remembering'. *Annu. Rev. Psychol.* 2022.73:187–215. (Ed.)

3. For examples of current research on sensory development as a prerequisite for cognitive development (and language development), see The Temporal Dynamics of Learning Center's overview of 'basic science' (https://tdlc.ucsd.edu/). (Ed.)

4. Wolfgang Köhler (1887–1967). German psychologist. Pioneer of Gestalt Psychology, together with Max Wertheimer (1880–1943) and Kurt Koffka (1886–1941). Emigrated to the US in 1935. Conducted observational experiments on problem solving by apes and showed

that chimpanzees are able to solve spatial problems by stacking crates and using sticks to access food that is out of reach. He saw the ways the apes arrived at their solutions as similar to basic human problem-solving processes and suggested that studying them could yield insights into learning and discovery processes that might be useful for education. (Ed.)

5. Bühler, *The Mental Development of the Child*. (KK)

6. Remplein, *Die seelische Entwicklung in der Kindheit und Reifezeit* (Mental Development in Childhood and Maturity). (KK)

7. Bühler, *The Mental Development of the Child*. (KK)

8. König is objecting here to a lack of distinction between an 'instinctive intelligence' that is displayed in a highly developed form by the apes, and the – in his view – categorically different type of intelligence represented by the free, human capacity of thinking, which emerges in a very simple form in a child's third year (as will be described) and leads to reflective self-consciousness and the ability to engage in cognitive deliberations that are not tied to the satisfaction of bodily desires and the solution of spatial-motor problems in their service. Unlike Köhler, König does not see the instinctive intelligence displayed by the apes as an early form or precursor of the latter, but as a separate phenomenon that does not belong to the same developmental trajectory. (Ed.)

9. As quoted by Remplein, *Die seelische Entwicklung in der Kindheit und Reifezeit* (Mental Development in Childhood and Maturity). (KK)

10. Here, again, König emphasises the distinction between cognitive functions that are tied to the precursors of thinking, such as sensory and motor activity, language and memory, and 'thinking' proper as an emancipated internal mental process at the thinker's free disposition. (Ed.)

11. Here, König finally spells out the distinction between instinctive or organic intelligence and the emancipated, self-conscious and deliberate, free capacity of thinking, which he has been building up throughout this section. (Ed.)

12. That is, in line with how the development of language has been characterised in the previous chapter, the syntax of a child's native language, living in the surrounding social environment, and its other structural properties are integrated and co-structure the child's evolving consciousness and experience, but are not yet themselves the subject of reflective awareness. Children embody them and experience themselves and the world *through* them. (Ed.)

13. In the German language, in which König wrote this text, all nouns have one of three genders and can take on four different syntactic

roles ('cases') as part of a sentence or phrase, changing articles and endings as they do so. Similar forms of declension occur in many language families around the world, including Andean, Bantu, Semitic, and Turkic languages, for example. They also existed in Old English but disappeared in the transition to modern English. (Ed.)

14. I have based my descriptions on the account in Homeyer, *Von der Sprache zu den Sprachen* (From Language to Languages). (KK)

15. Aristotle (384–22 BC) described ten categories, ten types of 'things', or aspects of reality, about which statements can be made: substance/ essence, quantity, quality, relative relation, place, time, position/ posture/attitude, state/condition, action, being affected. These categories are reflected in the syntax of language, which offers tools to grasp and express them. By learning to speak, children begin to operate on their experience in terms of these categories, helped by the structural scaffolding of the language, before they develop the capacity of thinking freely in these terms. (Ed.)

16. E. Köhler, *Die Persönlichkeit des dreijährigen Kindes* (The Personality of the Three-Year-Old Child). (KK)

17. The over-application of rules, which appears prior to mastery of exceptions, and is clearly not based on imitation, is cited by Chomsky as evidence for the acquisition of language as a rule-based system, based on variations of a universal grammar, which cannot be explained by behaviourist learning theory with its principle of operant conditioning through reinforcement (see notes in previous chapter). (Ed.)

18. Steiner, *Questions of Art and Life in the Light of Spiritual Science*. See lecture of July 17, 1915. (KK)

19. Elsa Köhler (1879–1940). Austrian developmental psychologist and educational reformer. Developed innovative methods for the study of didactic and learning processes in real-life classroom situations. Barred from academic work by the National-Socialist government after the annexation of Austria in 1938. (Ed.)

20. E. Köhler, *Die Persönlichkeit des dreijährigen Kindes* (The Personality of the Three-Year-Old Child). (KK)

21. Steiner, *Building Stones for an Understanding of the Mystery of Golgotha*, pp. 194f. (KK)

22. Steiner, *Human Evolution: A Spiritual-Scientific Quest*, p. 113. (KK)

23. Despite the development of memory being one of the oldest fields of study in the cognitive sciences, many processes remain poorly understood. However, it is generally accepted that the ability to form stable memories of events and access them at will at a later

time is established gradually, based on maturational processes that are only completed in adolescence. The phenomenon often referred to as infantile amnesia 'is unlikely to be explained by a unitary theory, with the protracted development of multiple brain regions and neurotransmitter systems important for learning and memory likely to be involved' (Madsen, H.B. and Kim, J.H. (2016). 'Ontogeny of memory: An update on 40 years of work on infantile amnesia'. *Behavioural Brain Research* Volume 298, Part A, 4–14). The authors point out that recent research has shifted the emphasis of theories of memory development from the question of memory formation towards greater interest in changes in the process of spontaneous forgetting. Thus, while contemporary studies continue to confirm that adults 'rarely recall events that occurred before the age of three and have spotty recollection of experiences that occurred between three and seven years of age' – the general picture of memory development that König's account is based on – children between five and ten frequently recall events that happened before they were one year old (and sometimes as young as one month). By the time they reach early adolescence, at age twelve or thirteen, however, children's memory no longer stretches back to the time before they turned one, and by the time they become adults, the earliest memory that remains accessible is typically of the time of around three years of age. This suggests that early memories – even episodic memories – may be formed, but do not 'crystallise' or stabilise to the same degree as later ones, 'dissolving' more quickly the earlier in development they occur. Consistent with the understanding of trauma as a lack of forgetting, the authors also observe that exposure to early life stress reduces infantile amnesia and leads to an earlier 'crystallisation' of memories, which remain accessible. All of this remains work in progress. (Ed.)

24. In his account of the evolution of human consciousness, Rudolf Steiner evokes the ancient myth of Atlantis to refer to what is generally understood to be the Upper Paleolithic period, prior to the end of the last Ice Age. Steiner's understanding of human consciousness and development during that period is complex and subject to different interpretations. A detailed account is not possible here. (Ed.)

25. What König, following Steiner, calls 'localised memory' can be understood as a form of implicit memory related to the phenomenon of 'priming'. Priming occurs when a particular sensory experience or pattern becomes familiar through prior exposure. This is the most primitive process of implicit, non-declarative memory. It evokes feelings and other responses, including impulses for action,

by association with the familiar perceptual stimulus. Defrancisco and Rovee-Collier (2008) have shown that priming in children up until nine months of age is dependent on a reproduction of the same stimulus in the same context, whereas between nine and twelve months of age, a priming stimulus can reactivate memories in a different context than that in which they originally occurred, representing a step in the maturation of memory capacity (see Defrancisco, B.S. and Rovee-Collier, C. (2008). 'The specificity of priming effects over the first year of life'. *Dev Psychobiol*. 2008, Jul; 50(5):486–501). Steiner links priming to the cultural practice of creating memorials and markers of places where important events have occurred (e.g., standing stones, cup and ring marks and other types of rock carvings). (Ed.)

26. Steiner, *World History and the Mysteries in the Light of Anthroposophy*, p. 8. (KK)

27. 'Rhythmical memory' is closely related to what is commonly known as 'procedural memory', a more complex form of implicit memory than priming. Procedural memory is established by actively repeating the production (or participation in the production) of an experience. The cultural practices of ritual, chant, dance and recitation, among others, build on these processes. Recent research has shown that sleep plays an important role in the consolidation of procedural memory, and there is some suggestion that it may be specifically the REM (dream) phase of sleep that occurs primarily in the second half of the night (and which is shared by some animals), which supports this type of memory. However, this has not yet been fully confirmed and slow-wave dreamless sleep (N2) may also be important (see Schönauer, M., Geisler, T. and Gais, S. (2014). 'Strengthening procedural memories by reactivation in sleep'. *J Cogn Neurosci*. 2014 Jan; 26(1):143–53.; Ackermann, S. and Rasch, B. (2014). 'Differential effects of non-REM and REM sleep on memory consolidation?' 2014 Feb; 14(2): 430). (Ed.)

28. Steiner, *World History and the Mysteries*, p. 10. (KK)

29. 'Time memory' is related to 'declarative memory', the conscious and deliberate form of memory that can be called up at will. Researchers distinguish two types of declarative memory: 'semantic memory' of facts and 'episodic memory' of past events. Steiner's concept of 'time memory' appears to refer primarily to episodic memory. There is strong evidence that slow-wave sleep (particularly the N2 stage of dreamless sleep that occurs primarily in the first half of the night and has only been detected in humans, not in animals) plays a key role in the consolidation of both types of declarative memory (see Ackermann, S. and Rasch, B. (2014). 'Differential effects of non-REM and REM sleep on memory

consolidation?' 2014 Feb; 14(2):430). (Ed.)

30. Steiner, *World History and the Mysteries*, pp. 10f. (KK)

31. Language is involved in rhythmical memory through repetition, rhyme, chant etc., and in time memory through the declarative and conceptual articulation of what is remembered. (Ed.)

32. Stern in his *Psychology of Early Childhood* gives an explanation of 'marking' and 'be-thinking' different from the above. It would lead us too far afield if we went into details here. (Ed.)

33. Bühler, *The Mental Development of the Child*, p. 314. (KK)

34. Stern, *Psychology of Early Childhood*, p. 207. (KK)

35. Stern, *Psychology of Early Childhood*, p. 240. (KK)

36. The importance of autobiographic memory (resulting from the increasing stability and continuity of episodic memory) for the development of self-awareness and a self-concept is affirmed by recent research. At the same time, the relationship is seen as bi-directional, so that the maturing of the self-concept (because of other maturational factors) is understood to be facilitating the formation of autobiographic memory. (See Ross, J.; Hutchison, J. & Cunningham, S.J. (2020). 'The me in memory: the role of the self in autobiographical memory development'. *Child Dev.* 2020 Mar;91(2):e299-e314). (Ed.)

37. Steiner, *The Foundations of Human Experience* (CW293), Anthroposophic Press, USA 1996, p. 55. Memory arises from the encounter – even confrontation – with an object or experience that is not produced by the self but is met as a given that becomes known through that confrontation. The inner pictures of fantasy, on the other hand, arise from the creative activity of the self and are its own production. Antipathy and sympathy are used here to characterise these different relationships, between I and not-I in the first case, and between the I and its own activity in the second. (Ed.)

38. Stern, *Psychology of Early Childhood*, p. 276. (KK)

39. Ibid., p. 185. 'Mental image' may be a better translation of the German term 'Vorstellung' than 'fantasy-percept', as what is meant here is not a 'percept' in the true sense. (Ed.)

40. The role of pretend play in child development continues to be a subject of research and debate. It appears to be a uniquely and universally human function that occurs naturally as part of a developmental schedule, based in organic maturation, and therefore is understood as evolutionary in origin by some (Lilliard, A.S. (2017). 'Why do children (pretend) play?' *Trends Cogn Sci.* 2017 Nov; 21(11):826–34). Its absence is a sign of developmental challenges and is particularly associated with autism spectrum disorders

(González-Sala, F. et al. (2021). 'Symbolic play among children with autism spectrum disorder: a scoping review'. *Children* (Basel) 2021 Sep 12; 8(9):801). Pretend play is clearly connected with the development of a number of important cognitive capacities, including symbolic thinking (as König describes here), theory of mind (the ability to imaginatively enter the other person's perspective) and counterfactual reasoning (the ability to think through hypothetical scenarios that are different from the directly experienced reality) (see Weisberg, D.S. (2015). 'Pretend play'. *Wiley Interdiscip Rev Cogn Sci.* 2015 May-Jun; 6(3):249–61); however, there is an ongoing debate around the degree to which it plays a causal role in the development of these capacities, or simply co-occurs with them (compare Lillard, A.S. et al. (2013). 'The impact of pretend play on children's development: a review of the evidence'. *Psychol Bull.* 2013 Jan; 139(1):1–34; and Weisberg, D.S., Hirsh-Pasek, K. and Golinkoff, R.M. (2013). 'Embracing complexity: rethinking the relation between play and learning: comment on Lillard et al'. (2013). *Psychol Bull.* 2013 Jan; 139(1): 35–39). (Ed.)

41. Stern, *Psychology of Early Childhood.* (KK)

42. On the connection of imaginative play with positive emotion, see Rao, Z. and Gibson, J.L. (2021). 'You pretend, I laugh: associations between dyadic pretend play and children's display of positive emotions'. *Front Psychol.* Jun 23; 12:669–767). (Ed.)

43. Lillard (2017, full reference above) also sees 'animal play fighting … as an analog [to human pretend play], as both activities involve as-if, metacommunicative signalling and symbolism,' even though in its specifics, true imaginative play is a uniquely human phenomenon. (Ed.)

44. Ernst von Feuchtersleben (1806–49). Austrian physician, poet and philosopher. Published pioneering texts on psychiatry and clinical psychology, as well as acclaimed collections of poetry and the early popular psychology 'self-help' book quoted here, *Diaetetik der Seele* (Dietetics of the Soul), advocating a harmonious lifestyle as a foundation of psychological wellbeing. (Ed.)

45. Feuchtersleben, *Diaetetik der Seele* (Dietetics of the Soul). See Chapter 3: Fantasy. (KK)

46. E. Köhler, *Die Persönlichkeit des dreijährigen Kindes* (The Personality of the Three-Year-Old Child), p. 67. (KK)

47. In paratactic languages, such as Chinese, the logical relationship between clauses is implied and has to be inferred from context, rather than being explicitly expressed through conjunctions or similar features, as in hypotactic languages. Connective elements,

when they do exist, are optional (Yu, N. (1993). 'Chinese as a paratactic language'. *Journal of Second Language Acquisition and Teaching 1*, 1–15). Many other non-Western languages (including, for example, Japanese, Korean, Turkic languages, various indigenous languages of the Amazon, North America, East Africa, and Melanesia) are 'clause chaining' languages, following a third option besides subordination of clauses (hypotaxis) and coordination of clauses (parataxis). In clause chaining, an almost unlimited number of clauses of a subordinate status are bracketed by a superordinate clause, which opens and closes the sentence. This requires significant planning and sustained attention of speakers and listeners, as the full meaning of a sentence only becomes available once all the medial clauses (which in some languages may have different subjects) have been completed and the closing bracket of the main clause has been uttered to finalise the sentence. Children growing up in these language systems typically begin to use two-clause sentences (one main clause, bracketing one subordinate clause) around the age of two or two-and-a-half. This is followed by a phase in which three to five clauses are chained together. Once this has been mastered, children begin to use unlimited medial clause chains. Children using these languages are managing less syntactic and analytical complexity, but instead longer sustained attention on more inclusive strings of circumstances and relationships that form an interconnected whole, than children growing up with hypotactic languages (Sarvasy, H.S. & Choi, S. (2020). 'Beyond the two-clause sentence: acquisition of clause chaining in six languages'. *Front Psychol.* 2020; 11: 1586). The study of how the qualities and challenges of different native languages affect early cognitive development and perhaps cognitive styles is still in its infancy. (Ed.)

48. Stern, *Psychology of Early Childhood,* p. 170. (KK)

49. E. Köhler, *Die Persönlichkeit des dreijährigen Kindes* (The Personality of the Three-Year-Old Child), p. 67. (KK)

50. The understanding of the beginnings of autobiographical memory and its emergence from 'the enigma' of infantile amnesia continues to be limited and is the subject of ongoing research (see Howe, M.L. (2019). 'Unraveling the nature of early (autobiographical) memory'. *Memory* 2019 Jan; 27(1):115–21). (Ed.)

51. Karl Rauch (1897–1966). German publisher, author and translator. Translated and published the works of Antoine de Saint-Exupéry (including *The Little Prince*) in German. (Ed.)

52. Rauch, *Der Schatten des Vaters* (Father's Shadow). (KK)

53. Moriz Carrière (1817–95). German philosopher, historian and art

historian. (Ed.)

54. Reichard, *Die Früherinnerung* (Early Memory). (KK)

55. Jean Paul (Johann Paul Friedrich Richter) (1763–1825). German Romantic author, humourist, and early activist for freedom of the press. His booklet 'Levana oder Erziehlehre' (Levana: Or, The Doctrine of Education) develops ideas for the reform of education. (Ed.)

56. Reichard, *Die Früherinnerung* (Early Memory). (KK)

57. One of the key motifs of Steiner's understanding of human development lies in the idea that the same forces that are initially involved in the growth and formation of a child's bodily organs, become available later, once the respective organs have reached (relative) functional maturity, as psychological, motoric, language and cognitive capacities at the child's free disposition. Ultimately, these forces originate in a spiritual world, in which the archetypes of the human body and its various organs are held, and on which the spiritual individuality of the child draws when building its body and individualising the forms of the earthly 'model' inherited from the parents. In relation to the capacities of walking, speaking, and thinking, Steiner elaborates this, for example, in his lectures in CW219 (November 26, 1922), GA224 (April 28–29, 1923), CW307 (August 10, 1923) and GA223 (August 30, 1923). The lectures contained in CW152 (especially March 7, 1914) explore deeper aspects connected with the spiritual archetype behind these developmental principles. (Ed.)

58. During this time, previously harmonious imaginative and symbolic peer play becomes more challenging: 'As the toddler develops his sense of self, exhibited by the emergence of possessive pronouns like "I", "me", "my", and "mine", play with peers often deteriorates swiftly and cannot be sustained due to constant conflict.' (Scott, H.K. and Cogburn, M. (2022). 'Peer play'. In: StatPearls [Internet]. Treasure Island (FL): StatPearls Publishing; 2022 Jan. 2022 Jul 4). (Ed.)

59. Adolf Busemann (1887–1967). German psychologist and educator. Made significant contributions to developmental psychology and linguistics. (Ed.)

60. Busemann, 'Erregungsphasen der Jugend' (Arousal Phases of Youth). (KK)

61. E. Köhler, *Die Persönlichkeit des dreijährigen Kindes* (The Personality of the Three-Year-Old Child), p. 232. (KK)

62. The 'higher self' or 'higher ego', as understood from an anthroposophical perspective, refers to the true spiritual individuality, which carries all of the individual's future possibilities

and potential beyond what can be realised in a single biography. The 'lower ego' is the earthly self-experience that comes about when the individuality becomes self-aware in the mirroring of its experiences within the limits of space, time and a bodily constitution, through which it experiences the world and itself as an agent in the world. By 'death' of the higher ego, König means that now the experience of oneself as a limited, earthly, and embodied self takes centre stage, occluding the awareness of the true higher self. (Ed.)

63. Steiner, *The Spiritual Guidance of the Individual and Humanity*, p. 8. (KK)

64. Remplein, *Die seelische Entwicklung in der Kindheit und Reifezeit* (Mental Development in Childhood and Maturity), p. 143. (KK)

65. Steiner, *The Spiritual Guidance of the Individual and Humanity*, p. 9. (KK)

66. Here, König alludes to the Prologue of the Gospel of John. Building on Steiner's spiritual-scientific characterisation of these developmental processes, he integrates the picture built up so far into a contemplative view of the incarnational process as a whole. This integrated contemplative understanding finds its central organising principle in the Platonic concept of the Logos as the source of all creative processes in the macrocosm (the universe) and the microcosm (the human being) alike, and the archetype of each individual human I. It is this I, of which the Prologue of the Gospel of John says that it was 'born, not of blood, but of God', so that 'mortals should become immortals', that is, become conscious of their true individuality beyond their limited earthly personality, and as 'temporal creatures [...] possess eternity', as the ninth century theologian John Scotus Eriugena elaborates in his meditation on the Prologue. For, 'as the great Dionysius the Areopagite says, "the being of all things is their superessential divinity."' (Eriugena, J.S. (1990). *The Voice of the Eagle: The Heart of Celtic Christianity*. Hudson: Lindisfarne Press). (Ed.)

67. In Steiner's Johannine understanding, the Christ-being is the universal Logos and appears as such in different religious and philosophical traditions by different names. It is distinct from the historical figure of Jesus (who is part of the complex story of humanity's relationship to the Logos), and not a denominationally bound concept. What Steiner (in agreement with Dionysius, Eriugena and others) means by 'Christ' is, seen from one particular vantage point, the spiritual archetype of the (higher) human I. (Ed.)

68. Steiner, *The Spiritual Guidance of the Individual and Humanity*, p. 18f. (KK)

Chapter 4. The Unfolding of the Three Highest Senses

1. Here, König returns to an issue that was already raised in the context of the second chapter, and which is addressed in the comments there from one angle, namely the distinction between the capacity to perceive auditory stimuli (the 'sense of hearing') and the capacity to perceive words *as* language (the 'sense of word'). The latter is involved, among other things, in speech-in-noise perception, i.e., the perceptual capacity to perceive and selectively attend to speech within a noisy environment. Now, König (following Steiner) introduces two further distinctions. The first distinguishes the capacity to perceive words as language ('sense of word') from the capacity to apprehend meaning *in* words and speech utterances, in the form of ideas and concepts ('sense of thought'). The second distinguishes this 'sense of thought' as a perceptual capacity from the capacity of 'thinking', which consists in the performance of mental operations on the objects (concepts) apprehended or perceived by means of the 'sense of thought', or in the creation of new concepts through the activity of the I in the mind. (Ed.)

2. Stern, *Psychology of Early Childhood,* p. 147. (KK)

3. Interesting lines of current research suggest, among other things, that speech-in-noise recognition is stronger in musicians (Hennessy, S., Mack, W.J. and Habibi, A. (2022). 'Speech-in-noise perception in musicians and non-musicians: a multi-level meta-analysis'. *Hear Res.* 2022 Mar 15; 416:108442) and impaired in individuals with dyslexia, where it can be improved by strengthening awareness of the rhythmical properties of speech (Hirtum, T.V., Ghesquière, P. and Wouters, J. (2021). 'A bridge over troubled listening: improving speech-in-noise perception by children with dyslexia'. *J Assoc Res Otolayngol.* 2021 Jul; 22(4): 465–80). (Ed.)

4. Edmund Husserl (1859–1938). German-Austrian philosopher and mathematician. Founder of modern phenomenology. Influenced many key movements in twentieth-century Continental European philosophy, psychology, consciousness studies, psychiatry and neurosciences. (Ed.)

5. Max Scheler (1874–1928). German phenomenologically oriented philosopher, anthropologist, and sociologist. (Ed.)

6. Scheler, *Abhandlungen und Aufsätze* (Treatises and Essays), Volume 1, pp. 329f. (KK)

7. Ludwig Binswanger (1881–1966). Swiss psychiatrist and pioneer of a phenomenological orientation in psychiatry and 'Daseinsanalyse' as a therapeutic approach. (Not to be confused with other eminent psychiatrists in the Binswanger family.) (Ed.)

FIRST THREE YEARS OF THE CHILD

8. Binswanger, *Ausgewählte Vorträge und Aufsätze: Band 2* (Selected Lectures and Articles: Volume 2). p. 308. (KK)

9. König asserts here that speech can be seen as having a bodily, a soul ('psychic' or experiential) and a spiritual (mental or cognitive) dimension, which are apprehended separately. The 'body' of a speech expression is its sound formation (or gestural formation, in the case of sign language). It is perceived by the 'sense of hearing', like other sound formations. The soul aspect of a speech expression is that which it carries as pure expression of an ensouled being. This is perceived, when the word is grasped *as* word, as expression (and not just as sound), by the 'sense of word'. The spiritual or mental dimension is its meaning, which is apprehended in the form of a concept. From a phenomenological perspective, this has to be understood also as a perceptual process, not an inferential one, as the meaning is beheld in a direct and immediate way (or not, when the process fails) through the 'sense of thought', not 'constructed' by the listener. Thus, all corresponding aspects of the human being are also involved in this process. (Ed.)

10. Steiner's theory of the senses is based on a phenomenology of the kinds of 'things' or aspects of reality that can be perceived (categories of perceptual objects). It takes its starting point from the structure of perceptual experience and identifies for each category of objects of perception a 'sense'. The nature and function of the sense organs or sensory systems, which make perception possible in relation to each category of experience, can then be investigated on this basis. In *Anthroposophy: A Fragment* (CW45), published in 1910 and based on lectures given in 1909, Steiner initially establishes ten such categories of perceptual experience (perception of the body's own state and wellbeing, the body's own movement, the body's state of balance in relation to space and gravity, smell, taste, light/colour, temperature, sound, language, and concepts). In 1916, he picks this theme up again, adding two more senses: the sense of touch, as the foundational body sense, and the sense of the I of another person (the ability to perceive the other person as a person). He now also sketches out the sense organ systems which, as parts of the nervous system, serve as bodily foundations for the ability to perceive each of these twelve aspects or categories of perceptual experience (see *Toward Imagination* (CW169) and *The Riddle of Humanity* (CW170)). (Ed.)

11. Steiner, *A Psychology of Body, Soul and Spirit: Anthroposophy, Psychosophy, Pneumatosophy*, pp. 17f. (KK)

12. For example, all the problems of the riddle of aphasia can be gradually brought nearer to a solution through these ideas, and from this starting point the burning questions of the disturbances

of reading and writing in childhood can be met with real understanding. (KK)

13. Franz Brentano (1838–1917). German philosopher in the Aristotelian tradition. Withdrew from the active Catholic priesthood in protest at the doctrine of papal infallibility. His work was foundational for the development of modern phenomenology by his student Edmund Husserl. Along with other significant twentieth-century thinkers, Rudolf Steiner also studied with Brentano in Vienna, possibly at the same time as Husserl. Brentano's work was of critical importance to Steiner and some of Steiner's most significant philosophical concepts, including his approach to the study of sense perception, result from his engagement with Brentano. Steiner's book *Riddles of the Soul* (CW21) is dedicated to Brentano. (Ed.)

14. 'Intentional relation' is a term coined by Brentano to describe the relation between a conscious subject and the objects of their consciousness. This concept became foundational to Husserl's phenomenology. (Ed.)

15. Steiner, *Riddles of the Soul* (CW21), Mercury Press, USA 1996, p 127. (KK)

16. That is, that the expressive 'word' quality of speech, as well as the concepts it carries, are not inferred on the basis of some indirect mental process occurring in the listener but are perceived directly. This view is in line with classical phenomenological perspectives in the Husserlian tradition and contemporary phenomenologically oriented neuroscientific approaches (e.g., Francisco Varela, Evan Thompson and Eleanor Rosch), but it conflicts with the psychophysical paradigm in the study of perception pioneered by Gustav Fechner (1801–87) and Hermann von Helmholtz (1821–94). This approach treats conscious perceptual experience as the indirect result of the processing of sensory stimuli by the organs of the sensory systems involved, and imagines the conscious observer as receiving the end product of this processing activity. Conscious experience is therefore seen as a construct of the perceiver. The latter view, though epistemologically fatally flawed (see Anthony Kenny's 'homunculus fallacy'), still underlies much of contemporary work in the neurophysiology of sense perception (e.g., the work of Richard L. Gregory). Steiner also deals with these problems from an epistemological point of view in his *The Philosophy of Spiritual Activity* (CW4). (Ed.)

17. This could also be translated as 'mental' or 'cognitive' development. (Ed.)

18. Charles Wilfred Valentine (1879-1964). British psychologist and

educator. (Ed.)

19. Valentine, *The Psychology of Early Childhood*, p. 393. (KK)

20. Ibid. (KK)

21. Ibid. (KK)

22. This progression from babbling as pure motor play towards imitation of the speech sounds heard in the surrounding is already addressed in the endnotes to Chapter 2. (Ed.)

23. Valentine, *The Psychology of Early Childhood*, p. 399. (KK)

24. William Thierry Preyer (1841–97). Physiologist and pioneer of experimental and empirical methods to study physiology and psychology. He made contributions to psychophysics and child development. He was born in England, and studied and worked in Germany. (Ed.)

25. Preyer, *Die Seele des Kindes* (The Child's Soul), p. 306. (KK)

26. Stern, *Psychology of Early Childhood*, p. 146. (KK)

27. Preyer, *Die Seele des Kindes* (The Child's Soul), p. 308. (KK)

28. In line with this, contemporary research also understands the development of phoneme recognition as a process in which auditory and visual perception play a joint role: 'Understanding spoken language is an audiovisual event that depends critically on the ability to discriminate and identify phonemes yet we have little evidence about the role of early auditory experience and visual speech on the development of these fundamental perceptual skills.' (Jerger, S. et al. (2017). 'Visual speech alters the discrimination and identification of non-intact auditory speech in children with hearing loss'. *Int J Pediatr Otorhinolaryngol.* 2017 Mar; 94:127–37). Though a need for more research is generally acknowledged, it appears that for hearing children, the role of visual perception in phoneme recognition becomes less critical after the third year, when children rely more strongly on the auditory channel for accuracy of recognition (see Erdener, D. and Burnham, D. (2018). 'Auditory-visual speech perception in three- and four-year-olds and its relationship to perceptual attunement and receptive vocabulary'. *J Child Lang*, 2018 Mar; 45(2): 273–89). Conversely, it has also been established that the visual influence on the understanding of heard speech at the meaning-level (as opposed to the phoneme level) increases with age from early to late childhood, both in noisy environments and in situations where speech is easily heard (see Irwin, J., Brancazio, L. and Volpe, N. (2017). 'The development of gaze to a speaking face'. *J Acoust Soc Am.* 2017 May; 141(5): 3145). This phenomenon may relate to what is described here as the 'sense of thought' (apprehension of meaning) and possibly also the 'sense

of I' (perception of the speaker as a self-conscious person with experiences, often discussed under the – from a phenomenological perspective inaccurate – heading of 'theory of mind'), which will be discussed below. (Ed.)

29. This is consistent with the observation that there is a gradual reduction in the reliance on lip-reading to support phoneme recognition after the initial developmental phase, at least in environments without noise interference. (Ed.)

30. That is, a perceptual capacity of discrimination precedes and lays the foundations for the development of judgment as an analytical cognitive process. (Ed.)

31. Steiner, *Anthroposophy: A Fragment*, p. 93. (KK)

32. The history of deaf education, particularly in the nineteenth and early twentieth centuries, saw a vigorous academic and politically charged debate between 'oralism' (the view that children should exclusively be taught lip-reading and oral speech) and 'manualism' (which saw sign language as the preferred route and discouraged the investment of time and energy in oral methods). It is now well established that sign languages are fully formed languages with all the features of human language, and that the early use of sign language does not interfere with, but supports the development of overall language skills – including acquisition of oral language – in deaf children, even in those with cochlear implants. Sign language provides access to a full language experience and environment in the critical period of the first three years, whereas the full experience of all features of language via the oral route is severely limited, depending on the degree of hearing loss. With the acquisition of sign language as a first language, parallel to the development of oral language, children grow up in a bimodal-bilingual environment, ensuring that at least one language can be fully accessed, so that the foundations for language and later cognitive development (as described throughout this book) can be laid (see Humphries, T. et al. (2019). 'Support for parents of deaf children: Common questions and informed, evidence-based answers'. *Int J Pediatr Otorhynolaryngol*. 2019 Mar; 118:134–42). (Ed.)

33. Valentine, *The Psychology of Early Childhood*, p. 414. (KK)

34. Indeed, the sense of word can also perceive the presence of language in these other media, independent of the auditory medium, as is shown in both visual speech reading and sign language. This only serves to underline the justification of recognising it as a distinct perceptual capacity, independent of the auditory sense. (Ed.)

35. Steiner, *Anthroposophy: A Fragment*, p. 94. (KK)

36. What exists today as 'Gestalt' psychology, frequently quite

misunderstood, has its roots here in the sense of speech. This, however, can be discussed only in a much wider setting. (KK)

37. Stern, *Psychology of Early Childhood*, p. 165. (KK)

38. Steiner, *Anthroposophy: A Fragment*, p. 94. (KK)

39. Valentine, *The Psychology of Early Childhood*, p. 420. (KK)

40. Quoted from Kainz, *Psychologie der Sprache* (Psychology of Language), Volume 2, p. 52. (KK)

41. Helen Keller (1880–1968). American author, lecturer, and activist. After losing her sight and hearing at nineteen months, she developed her own simple sign communication system. Her teacher Anne Sullivan facilitated her acquisition of full language through a touch-based sign language. After obtaining a university degree, she became an author and activist for disability rights, women rights, civil rights and peace. (Ed.)

42. Anne Sullivan (1866–1936). American educator. Teacher and lifelong friend of Helen Keller. (Ed.)

43. Quoted from Schmitt, *Helen Keller und die Sprache* (Helen Keller and Language). (KK)

44. See also K. König, *Die Geistgestalt Helen Keller* (The Spirit Figure of Helen Keller). (KK)

45. These perceptual experiences of one's own body are the subject of the 'sense of life', the 'sense of balance', and the 'sense of movement' respectively. In current scientific terminology, they are usually referred to as 'nociception', 'equilibrioception' and '(motor) proprioception' or 'kinaesthesia'. They are part of the 'somatosensory system', which facilitates an experience of the body, together with the 'sense of touch' or 'haptic sense'. In current scientific models of the sensory system, the 'sense of warmth' is also often included as a somatic sense, whereas Steiner and König categorise it among the senses concerned primarily with an experience of the outer environment (also referred to as the 'middle senses', which include smell (olfaction), taste (gustation) and sight (vision)). The 'higher senses' discussed here by König and Steiner are, except for hearing, typically not named as part of the 'sensory system' in the narrow sense, since many mainstream models assume that the experiences they facilitate involve inferential cognitive processes. However, as has already been pointed out, phenomenologically oriented approaches to psychology and neuroscience recognise the experiences of language, concepts, and the personhood of the other as primary perceptual phenomena. This question of what is 'sensory' and what is the outcome of further processing of perceptions is the backdrop to König's

reflections here. (Ed.)

46. In philosophy, the Latin term *ens* means a 'thing' or 'being', the essence of an entity, to which its name refers (as opposed to a quality or attribute *of* an entity). (Ed.)

47. This is an exaggeration in two respects. As recently as 2020, a set of hitherto unknown minute glands, now named the 'tubarial glands', were discovered by Dutch scientists at the intersection of nose and throat. Also, as is clear from the footnotes in Chapter 2, at least *some* aspects of the neurological systems involved in speech perception and comprehension were known, even before König's time (and he was aware of these). Nevertheless, it is true that the understanding of the organic basis of the three 'higher senses' or 'social senses' discussed here is still far more limited than that of the other senses, despite significant contributions made in recent decades, which, like the discovery of the tubarial glands, are often the result of advances in imaging technologies. Chief among these is the discovery, discussed further below, and first described in 1992, of 'mirror neurons' – variously described as 'the most hyped concept in neuroscience' (Jarrett, C.B. (2012). 'Mirror neurons: the most hyped concept in neuroscience?'. *Psychol. Today* [Blog]) or a game-changing 'point of no return in social and affective neuroscience' (Bonini, L. et al. (2022). 'Mirror neurons 30 years later: implications and applications'. *Trends Cogn Sci.* 2022 Sep; 26(9): 767–81). (Ed.)

48. Steiner, *Riddles of the Soul*, p. 127. (KK)

49. In other words, König is proposing that, in the case of the 'higher' or 'social senses' concerned primarily with the perception of intersubjective processes, the search needs to be for functionally interconnected sensory organ systems, rather than highly localised sense organs, as is the case especially for some of the 'middle' senses. A major step towards more precisely identifying such distributed sensory systems for perceptions that occur between self and other was made with the discovery of 'mirror neurons', and the broader phenomenon of 'mirror mechanisms' mapped across many different regions of the central nervous system. Among the key findings from this research, the following are particularly relevant for the present topic: distributed among virtually all areas of the brain involved in somatic movement (typically voluntary movements involving skeletal muscles, including those used in walking, speech production, gestures and facial expression) and visceral movement (regulation of involuntary movement of the internal organs, including heartbeat, constriction of blood vessels, and digestive processes), there are neurons that show the same activity when observing someone else move, act or react, as they

would if the self was producing the same action. While some of these neurons ('mirror neurons' in the narrow sense) simply participate in the embodied action or expression of the other in an imitative way, other neurons belonging to the 'mirror mechanism' allow the perceiver to either engage in, or inhibit, actual active imitation, or to initiate a different, but complementary response to the observed action, that is nevertheless closely in tune with the other. Thus, mirror mechanisms throughout the various brain areas and functional domains (movement, language, emotional, somatic, and visceral self-regulation) establish a kind of resonant coupling, or 'neuronal tuning', between self and other in a perception-action feedback loop. This feedback loop is not fixed but fluid and malleable according to the intentions and self-regulatory capacities of each partner. This is understood to be fundamental to social perception and interaction in the domains of coordinated motor action, imitation, language, communication, joint attention, imitation, empathy, emotional attunement, embodied cognition, and understanding of the intentions, decisions, motivations, beliefs, and actions of the other. In each functional system, other-selective neurons and neurons involved in self-monitoring and self-regulation are intimately intermingled, with some neurons involved in both aspects of the process (Bonini, L. et al. (2022). 'Mirror neurons 30 years later: implications and applications'. *Trends Cogn Sci.* 2022 Sep; 26(9): 767–81). The developmental processes that leads to the establishment of the mirror neuron system, and the time sequences involved, including maturational and/or adaptive and associative learning process that might play a role in early childhood, are still largely unknown (see also Kilner, J.M. and Lemon, R.N. (2013) 'What we know currently about mirror neurons'. *Curr Biol.* 2013 Dec 2; 23(23): R1057–R1062). (Ed.)

50. See also the detailed expositions by the author, 'Der Motorische Nerv wird entthront' ('The Motor Nerve is Dethroned') and 'Die Nerventätigkeit' ('Nerve Activity'). (KK)

51. The pyramidal system continues to be understood as the central integrating structure of the cortical sensory-motor system, which supports the integration of motor proprioception (sense of movement) and control of voluntary and deliberate motor activity (i.e., the feedback loop discussed in the notes on Chapter 1). It includes efferent nerves that run from the somatic movement areas of the cortex in front of the central cerebral groove to a midline crossing in the medulla oblongata, the lower part of the brain stem, and connect with the efferent neurons in the spinal cord that then branch out to the different muscle groups. Running in the opposite

direction, afferent nerves originating in the muscles gather in the spinal cord, also crossing over the midline in the brain stem, and then spread out over the somatic sensory cortex that lies behind the central groove and mirrors the motor cortex in its mapping of the skeletal-muscular system of the entire body (the so-called sensory and motoric 'homunculi'). The secondary and tertiary motor and sensory areas of the cortex lie forwards and backwards respectively of these primary motor and sensory maps. However, it is understood today that the subcortical motor system, which lies below the cortex and includes multiple different subcortical structures, plays a role that is much more intimately interconnected with cortical functions than previously thought. These subcortical structures are particularly involved in the formation of habitual movement patterns through practice and their stabilisation as skills that become 'automatic', that is, self-organising and no longer requiring deliberate intentional control (see Rohen, J.W. (2011). *Functional Morphology: The Dynamic Wholeness of the Organism.* Hillsdale: Adonis Press.) (Ed.)

52. That is to say, the core functions involved in walking, once established and stabilised, are integrated and maintained by the self-regulatory processes of the subcortical motor system, thus making the cortical structures of the pyramidal system available to support new conscious tasks. The cortical motor system, of course, also includes those cortical areas involved in the motor production of speech, with their centre in Broca's area in the (usually) left frontal lobe. Since the discovery of the mirror neuron processes, which occur in all cortical motor areas, it has become increasingly clear that so-called motor areas also serve a sensory function, namely the 'remapping of other-related information onto primarily self-related brain structures … with a major role in social cognition and guiding social interaction' (Bonini et al. 2022, cited above), that is to say, the resonant perception of embodied expressions of the other through the same system, which serves the self-regulation of one's own embodied expression in the same domain. In this light König (and Steiner) can be understood as suggesting that developmentally, the maturing pyramidal system in the first year is primarily occupied with the regulation and integration of a child's own movement, whereas thereafter it is 'freed up' and its function can shift towards sensory mirror mechanisms, which serve the perception of the other – including in the production of speech. While this goes beyond what can be ascertained based on existing empirical research, and while many details remain open, it is not inconsistent with the trends that result from the discoveries of the last decades. (Ed.)

53. Steiner, *The Riddle of Humanity*, p. 194. (KK)
54. Ibid. (KK)
55. Klaus Conrad (1905–961). German neurologist and psychiatrist. (Ed.)
56. Conrad, 'New Problems of Aphasia'. *Brain*. 1954 Dec; 77(4): 491–509. (KK)
57. Compare the footnotes in Chapter 1. (Ed.)
58. Steiner, *The Riddle of Humanity*, p. 196. (KK)
59. While not exactly the same, this account certainly resonates strongly with the characterisation of the mirror mechanisms, which consist in movements that are inwardly enacted in the nervous system as if they were being produced, but held back from actual production with no engagement of the muscles, and that thereby facilitate understanding of, and an ability to orient and respond to, the embodied expression of the other. (Ed.)
60. The German sociologist Hartmut Rosa offers a comprehensive concept of 'resonance' as a way of understanding the embodied human relationship to the world, which includes a discussion of intersubjectivity, perception and the body. Commenting on the role of mirror neurons, he remarks that '[the] insight that not only the relationship between subject and social world, but also the internal organisation of perception, thought, and action as well as the interplay between brain and organism can be properly comprehended only according to the logic of resonant processes is ... critical to understanding human relationships to the world' (p.147). Rosa's work offers highly fruitful possibilities for building bridges between contemporary neuroscience, phenomenology, and Steiner's spiritual-scientific perspective, which cannot be developed further here, but would make a good subject for further research. (Rosa, H. (2019). *Resonance: A Sociology of Our Relationship to the World*. Cambridge: Polity Press.) (Ed.)
61. Steiner, *The Riddle of Humanity*, p. 195f. (KK)
62. As König states, the nerves that innervate the muscles of the larynx are branches of the vagus nerve, the tenth cranial nerve. The vagus nerve is the longest nerve of the autonomous nervous system, with a central integrating function that supports parasympathetic ('rest and regeneration' mode) regulation of visceral functions of nearly all internal organs from the neck down to the upper part of the colon. In bundles afferent and efferent pathways terminate in various different parts of the brain on the one end, and via its lower branches, in the respective organ systems on the other. As part of the cranio-sacral system, it is complemented by the sacral nerves of the

parasympathetic system, which innervate the remaining lower organs, whereas the sympathetic nervous system reaches the organs via the spinal column to regulate their functions in high activity and energy consumption modes (sometimes referred to as 'fight or flight'). These parasympathetic functions are autonomous (vegetative) and involve visceral muscles outside of conscious control. The pathways innervating the parasympathetic functions in the organs, which make up the bulk of the vagus nerve, are, as König states, not connected with the pyramidal system supporting voluntary movement. They are rooted in the lower brain regions, the limbic system, and the hypothalamus, which regulate vegetative functions. However, the upper motor neurons leading to the voluntarily controlled muscles of the larynx do originate in the cortical motor areas, from where they bundle in the nucleus ambiguus in the medulla oblongata (together with parasympathetic pathways to the heart and lungs) to join the vagus nerve (see Coverdell, T.C. et al. (2022). 'Genetic encoding of an oesophageal motor circuit'. *Cell Rep.* 2022 Jun 14; 39(11): 110962; and Sanders, I. et al. (1993). 'The innervation of the human larynx'. *Arch Otolaryngol Head Neck Surg.* 1993 Sep; 119(9): 934–39). While the details of the organisation of different pathways in the vagus nerve are still poorly understood (see Thompson, N., Mastitskaya, S. and Holder, D. (2019). 'Avoiding off-target effects in electrical stimulation of the cervical vagus nerve: neuroanatomical tracing techniques to study fascicular anatomy of the vagus nerve'. *J Neurosci Methods.* 2019 Sep 1; 325: 108325), the general picture that emerges is that the muscles of the larynx form an island of voluntary movement, embedded within the autonomic system of unconscious organic self-regulation. The cricothyroid muscle at the bottom of the larynx, which tenses and elongates the vocal cords, thus modulating pitch, is primarily innervated by the superior laryngeal nerve, which branches off from the vagus nerve above the larynx and connects with it in a downward-branching gesture. All the remaining muscles are primarily innervated by the recurrent laryngeal nerve, which branch off much lower and loop underneath the aorta (just above the heart) on the left and the subclavian artery (just above the lungs) on the right, before connecting with the larynx in an upward-branching gesture. This anatomical 'detour' through the realms of heart and lung, together with the special character of the muscles of the heart, which occupies a unique intermediary role between voluntary skeletal muscles and involuntary visceral muscles, and which also receives its parasympathetic innervation from the vagus nerve, supports the picture that the larynx is situated in a middle space, between conscious (voluntary) and unconscious (autonomic) bodily functions, where it creates an island of voluntary motor activity in the production of voice and speech (compare also

Rohen 2011, cited above). (Ed.)

63. Rudolf Treichler (1909–94). German anthroposophical physician and psychiatrist. (Ed.)

64. Treichler, 'Von der Welt des Lebenssinnes' ('From the World of Meaning in Life'). (KK)

65. Steiner, *The Riddle of Humanity*, p. 193f. (KK)

66. Rudolf Max Hess (1913–2007). Swiss neurologist. The characterisation of the sympathetic and parasympathetic parts of the autonomous nervous system formulated here still corresponds to current generally accepted understanding. (Ed.)

67. Quoted from Kroetz, 'Allgemeine Physiologie der autonomen nervösen Correlationen' (General Physiology of the Autonomic Nervous Correlations) (KK)

68. Treicher, 'Von der Welt des Lebenssinnes' ('From the World of Meaning in Life'). (KK)

69. Another way of asking this question, in the light of recent trends to recognise phenomena of resonance on multiple levels of the nervous system, would be: while it is clear that those aspects of the vagus nerve system that connect with upper motor neurons and cortical areas participate in the other-directed resonant mirror mechanisms described earlier, and can therefore be thought of as part of a sensory system for interpersonal/social perception, how is it with the genuinely autonomic/parasympathetic pathways that centre in the lower parts of the brain, especially the limbic system? Do these also have a similar sensory-resonant capacity? This question – which König explores here – remains unanswered in contemporary neuroscience. However, there are some conceptual developments that point in this direction. It has become clear that the connection between movement observation (movement of other) and motor imagery (internally rehearsed movement that is not acted out) on the one hand, and autonomic nervous system (ANS) activation on the other, is much more intimate and wide-ranging than previously thought, and that the ANS is resonantly involved in all motor observation and motor imagery. That means that through the medium of physical expression (movement, gesture, voice, facial expression…), the body participates not only in the physical formation of the other's movement expressions, but also in the autonomic visceral processes that accompany these (see Collet, C. et al. (2013). 'Autonomic nervous system correlates in movement observation and motor imagery'. *Front Hum Neurosci.* 2013; 7: 415). This is confirmed by the finding that, for example, breathing is modulated through ANS involvement in walking, but also in the observation and imagination of walking, when the mirror

neuron system is active without corresponding expressed motor activity (Pellicano et al. (2021). 'Respiratory function modulated during execution, observation and imagination of walking via SII'. *Sci Rep.* 2021; 11: 23752). Also, during sleep, CNS and ANS activity is coupled dynamically in mutually responsive ways that were not previously understood (de Zambotti. M. et al. (2018). 'Dynamic coupling between the central and autonomic nervous system during sleep: a review'. *Neurosci Biobehav Rev.* 2018 Jul; 90: 84–103). (Ed.)

70. A recent theory that takes this line of research further and has become influential in ideas on therapy (especially relating to trauma), is the so-called 'Polyvagal Theory' formulated by Stephen Porges (Porges, S.W. (2009). 'The polyvagal theory: New insights into adaptive reactions of the autonomic nervous system'. *Cleve Clin J Med.* 2009 Apr; 76 (Suppl 2): S86–S90). Building on questions that were left open by Hess (whom König cites here), and drawing on more recent empirical evidence and theoretical considerations, Porges proposes that the myelinated part of the human vagus nerve (which originates in the nucleus ambiguus and includes the laryngeal nerves as well as the nerve serving the heart) supports a third distinct autonomic sub-system with more advanced evolutionary origins than the basic sympathetic (mobilisation, fight-flight) and parasympathetic (immobilisation, death-feigning) functions in the traditional binary concept of the ANS. This third function is described as a social communication or social engagement system, which can operate when neither of the other two subsystems are active, because the environment is perceived as safe (via an embodied process that Porges calls 'neuroception', a kind of sensory monitoring process that takes place below the threshold of consciousness in the limbic system, where the sympathetic and parasympathetic functions flow together). The social engagement system supports visceral homeostasis (especially through the maintenance of a calm heart rate and breathing) as a foundation for the activities underlying embodied resonant engagement between self and other (including controlled gaze, facial expression, voice, listening etc.). While the polyvagal framework is not universally accepted, it seems to provide a promising avenue to further pursue the line of inquiry presented here by König. (Ed.)

71. The concept of the total autonomic nervous system as an anatomical physiological unity is today generally accepted. Stöhr, for example, writes: 'Results of anatomical investigations justify the assumption that the whole of the sympathetic system is a closed one, from which the outermost parts are sunk as independent little branches into the epithelial gland and muscle cells which they have to supply and form an inseparable physiological and

anatomical unit or they complete their course as differently shaped sensitive terminals.' (Stöhr, *Mikroskopische Anatomie des vegetativen Nervensystems* (Microscopic Anataomy of the Autonomic Nervous System), Berlin 1928). (KK)

72. With the nuclei in the brain stem, in particular the nucleus ambiguus, as key crossing points. (Ed.)

73. As described above, the voluntary motor pathways innervating the muscles of the larynx form the part of the vagus nerve that is most directly connected upwards, all the way into the cortical motor areas where the mirror neuron processes are found. Here, via the nucleus ambiguus in the brain stem, they lead over into the upper part of the pyramidal system where the laryngeal movements of self and other resonate. This allows them to be perceived and apprehended consciously by the self, which inwardly participates in the activity of the formative forces involved in the production of speech. (Ed.)

74. In this section, I have refrained quite intentionally from discussing the exposition given by H.E. Lauer in the fifth chapter of his fundamental book *Twelve Senses of Man*. There an attempt is also made to describe the physical organs of the 'higher' senses. Such a discussion here would become needlessly long and would be of interest to only a limited number of the readers for whom this book is meant. (KK)

75. Steiner, *Toward Imagination*, p. 53. (KK)

76. Steiner, *The Foundations of Human Experience*, p. 140. (KK)

77. A structurally very similar description of this perceptual process was developed by Edmund Husserl's student Edith Stein (1891–1942) in her doctoral dissertation, 'On the problem of empathy', the first comprehensive phenomenological treatment of the phenomenon of empathy ('Einfühlung'), published in 1917 (English translation: Stein, E. (1989). *On the Problem of Empathy*. Washington, DC: ICS Publications). Her work is still considered an important point of reference for phenomenologically oriented neuroscience (see Thompson, E. (2007). *Mind in Life: Biology, Phenomenology, and the Sciences of the Mind*. Cambridge, MA: Harvard University Press; and Lanzoni, S. (2018). *Empathy: A History*. New Haven, CT: Yale University Press.). Born Jewish, Edith Stein later became a Carmelite nun, was imprisoned and killed in Auschwitz, and is considered a saint in the Roman Catholic church. (Ed.)

78. In contemporary literature on child development, the capacity to perceive the other person as a self-aware person with a viewpoint and experiences other than one's own is usually referred to as 'theory of

mind'. From a phenomenological perspective, this is an inaccurate term, as it suggests that awareness of the personhood or 'I-hood' of the other is the indirect outcome of an inferential cognitive process – a kind of 'theory' that children develop, positing the existence of other ensouled I-beings. The phenomenological tradition, including Steiner and König, recognises that the experience of the I-hood of the other arises as a direct, unmediated perceptual experience, hence the 'sense of I'. Only when this breaks down, as can be the case in autism, inferential cognitive processes ('theories of mind') may be used as a replacement, in an effort to make sense of the intentions and actions of the other. (Ed.)

79. E. Köhler, *Die Persönlichkeit des dreijährigen Kindes* (The Personality of the Three-Year-Old Child), p. 110. (KK)

80. Wilhelm Hansen (dates unknown). German educational psychologist. Taught at Pädagogische Hochschule (University of Education) Vechta from 1947 to 1968. (Ed.)

81. Hansen, *Die Entwicklung des kindlichen Weltbildes* (The Development of the Child's Worldview), p. 211. (KK)

82. Remplein, *Die seelische Entwicklung in der Kindheit und Reifezeit* (Mental Development in Childhood and Maturity), p. 145. (KK)

83. This assumption, which is offered here without any grounding in empirical observations, rests on the image of the traditional father and mother roles in Western cultures. It can be complemented by the assumption that reality is a lot more complex and fluid, especially in a time when people of all genders are increasingly valuing the ability to express both masculine and feminine aspects of their personalities, and emancipate themselves from one-sided gender norms, including in their relationships to their children. Thus, both mothers and fathers can (and should!) embody and represent for the child the demands of an objective reality, and a protective holding and embracing gesture. (Ed.)

84. Steiner, *The Renewal of Education*, pp. 137f. (KK)

85. Steiner, *The Foundations of Human Experience*, p. 139. (KK)

86. Steiner, *The Riddle of Humanity*, p. 193. (KK)

87. The embodied human being as a whole, within the integrating experience of the sense of touch, and with all the known and potentially yet unknown capacities of their nervous system to mirror and resonate with the embodied presence of another I, is the sense organ for the 'I-sense'. This view of the body as a resonant instrument of perception is broadly consistent with the trends and directions of recent research on mirror neurons, resonance and empathy that have been cited throughout the endnotes here,

offering a promising framework for further research and deepened understanding of the processes involved. (Ed.)

88. The function of the pineal gland continues to be poorly understood. It is involved in the regulation of the waking and sleeping rhythm, inhibits the development of the reproductive organs during childhood, and appears to be involved in regulating bone development. Hormones from the pituitary gland are involved in maturation and activation of the reproductive organs, growth, and other metabolic functions. (Ed.)

89. The three higher senses are gateways into a perception of supersensible phenomena – words, thoughts and the other's I – though initially we take hold of them in and through their embodied expression. In doing so, they allow embodied existence to become transparent, to become a sense organ for the supersensible, and for human beings to become aware of themselves as spiritual beings in that embodied supersensible reality. Or as Lanzoni (2018, cited above, p. 280) says in the conclusion of her study of the history of empathy (an expression of 'I-sense'): 'Empathy, in its many varieties, offers an oblique and sometimes direct challenge to the idea that we are enclosed selves, sharply defined against the world and others ... Empathy dares us to move beyond the habitual borders of the self to reach toward another human being, animal, art object, or the natural world. We need the self to empathise, but we also have to leave it behind. This is one of empathy's mysteries, but it is also its promise.' (Ed.)

90. Novalis, *Hymns to the Night*. (KK)

91. Novalis (Friedrich von Hardenberg) (1772–1801). German (early) Romantic author, poet and philosopher; also lawyer, geoscientist and mining engineer. (Ed.)

Picture Credits

p.118: From *Gray's Anatomy* by Henry Gray and Henry Vandyke Carter.

p.125: From *Gray's Anatomy*.

p.127: From *Gray's Anatomy*.

Bibliography

Binswanger, L. *Ausgewählte Vorträge und Aufsätze*, Volume 2, Bern 1955.

Brock, J. *Biologische Daten für den Kinderarzt*, Volume 2, Berlin 1934.

Bühler, K. *The Mental Development of the Child*. London 1930.

Busemann, A. 'Erregungsphasen der Jugend', *Zeitschrift für Kinderforschung*, No. 33. 1927.

Conrad, K. 'New Problems of Aphasia', *Brain*, Volume 77, 1954.

Gehlen, A. *Der Mensch. Seine Natur und seine Stellung in der Welt*, Bonn 1950.

Hamann, *Des Ritters von Rosencreuz letzte Willensmeinung*.

Hansen, W. *Die Entwicklung des kindlichen Weltbildes*, Munich 1949.

Homeyer, H. *Von der Sprache zu den Sprachen*, Olten 1947.

Kainz, F. *Psychologie der Sprache*. Volume 2, Stuttgart 1943.

Köhler, E. *Die Persönlichkeit des dreijährigen Kindes*, Leipzig 1936.

Köhler, W. *The Mentality of Apes*, London/New York 1927.

König, K. 'Die Geistgestalt Helen Keller', *Das seelenpflegebedürftige Kind*, Volume 3, No. 1, 1956.

—, 'Der Motorische Nerv wird entthront', *Die Drei*, No. 1, 1955.

—, 'Die Nerventätigkeit kann nur durch eine Methode der Ausschliessung erfasst werden', *Beiträge zu einer Erweiterung der Heilkunst*, No. 3/4, 1955.

Kroetz, C. 'Allgemeine Physiologie der autonomen nervösen Correlationen', *Handbuch der normalen und pathologischen Physiologie,* Volume 16, No. 2, Berlin 1931.

Magnus, R. & de Kleijn, A. 'Körperstellung, Gleichgewicht und Bewegung', *Handbuch der normalen und pathologischen Psychologie,* Volume 15.1, Berlin 1930.

Novalis, *Hymns to the Night,* Translated by Mabel Cotterell.

Portmann, A. *Biologische Fragmente zu einer Lehre vom Menschen,* Basel 1944.

Porzig, W. *Das Wunder der Sprache,* Bern 1950.

Preyer, W. *Die Seele des Kindes,* Leipzig 1900.

Rauch, K. *Der Schatten des Vaters,* Esslingen 1954.

Reichard, H. *Die Früherinnerung,* Halle 1926.

Remplein, H. *Die seelische Entwicklung in der Kindheit und Reifezeit,* Munich 1950.

Scheler, M. *Abhandlungen und Aufsätze,* Volume 1, Leipzig 1915.

Schmitt, A. 'Helen Keller und die Sprache', *Münstersche Forschungen,* No.8, Münster 1954.

Sigismund, R. *Kind und Welt,* Braunschweig 1897.

Steiner, Rudolf. Volume Nos refer to the Collected Works (CW) available in English, or to the German Gesamtausgabe (GA).

—, *Anthroposophy: A Fragment* (CW45), Anthroposophic Press, New York 1996.

—, *Building Stones for an Understanding of the Mystery of Golgotha* (CW175), Rudolf Steiner Press, UK 2015.

—, *The Foundations of Human Experience* (formerly *Study of Man*) (CW293), Anthroposophic Press, USA 1996.

—, *The Riddle of Humanity* (CW170), Rudolf Steiner Press, UK 1990.

—, *The Karma of Untruthfulness: Volume 1* (CW173), Rudolf Steiner Press, UK 1988.

—, *Transforming the Soul: Volume 2* (CW59), Steiner Press, UK 1983.

—, *The Realm of Language* (from GA162), Mercury Press, USA 1984.

—, *The Renewal of Education Through the Science of the Spirit* (CW301), Steiner School Fellowship, UK 1981.

—, *Spiritual Guidance of the Individual and Humanity* (CW15), Anthroposophic Press, USA 1991.

—, *Riddles of the Soul* (CW21), Mercury Press, USA 1996.

—, *Toward Imagination* (CW169), Anthroposophic Press, USA 1990.

—, *A Psychology of Body, Soul and Spirit* (CW115), Anthroposophic Press, USA 1999.

—, *World History and the Mysteries in the Light of Anthroposophy* (CW233), Rudolf Steiner Press, UK 2021.

—, *Die Wissenschaft vom Werden des Menschen,* (GA183), Dornach, 1967.

Stern, William. *Psychology of Early Childhood,* 2 ed., London 1930.

Stifter, Adalbert. *Betrachtungen und Bilder,* Vienna 1923.

Stöhr, *Mikroskopische Anatomie des vegetativen Nervensystems,* Berlin 1928.

Storch, O. *Die Sonderstellung des Menschen im Lebensabspiel und Vererbung,* Vienna 1948.

Treichler, R. 'Von der Welt des Lebenssinnes', *Beiträge zur Erweiterung der Heilkunst,* No. 7/8, 1952.

Valentine, C.W. *The Psychology of Early Childhood,* London 1947.

Index

About the Editor

Dr Jan Goeschel is the founding President of the Camphill Academy, the higher education organisation of the Camphill Movement in North America. He has a PhD in Special Needs Education and Rehabilitation Sciences from the University of Cologne, Germany. He previously worked as a class teacher for children and adolescents with intellectual and developmental disabilities at the Beaver Run Camphill School in Pennsylvania, USA, where he still lives.

Karl König's collected works are being published in English by Floris Books and in German by Verlag Freies Geistesleben. They encompass the entire, wide-ranging literary estate of Karl König, including his books, essays, manuscripts, lectures, diaries, notebooks, his extensive correspondence and his artistic works, across twelve subjects.

Karl König Archive subjects

Medicine and study of the human being
Curative education and social therapy
Psychology and education
Agriculture and science
Social questions
The Camphill movement
Christianity and the festivals
Anthroposophy
Spiritual development
History and biographies
Artistic and literary works
Karl König's biography

Karl König Archive
www.karlkoeniginstitute.org
office@karlkoeniginstitute.org

Floris
Books

For news on all our **latest books,**
and to receive **exclusive discounts,**
join our mailing list at:

florisbooks.co.uk

Plus subscribers get a FREE book
with every online order!

We will never pass your details to anyone else.

Printed in the USA
CPSIA information can be obtained
at www.ICGtesting.com
JSHW011620020823
45826JS00002B/12

9 781782 508472